Key Competencies for a Successful Life and a Well-Functioning Society

Key Competencies

for a Successful Life and a Well-Functioning Society

Edited by
Dominique Simone Rychen
Laura Hersh Salganik

Hogrefe & Huber

KH

Library of Congress Cataloging-in-Publication Data

is now available via the Library of Congress Marc Database under the

LC Control Number: 2003107492

National Library of Canada Cataloguing-in-Publication

Rychen, Dominique S.
  Key competencies for a successful life and a well-functioning society / Dominique Simone Rychen, Laura Hersh Salganik.

Includes bibliographical references.
ISBN 0-88937-272-1

  1. Life skills. 2. Core competencies. I. Salganik, Laura Hersh II. Title.

HQ2037.R92 2003   646.7   C2003-903251-5

Copyright © 2003 by Hogrefe & Huber Publishers

PUBLISHING OFFICES
USA: Hogrefe & Huber Publishers, 44 Brattle Street, 4th Floor,
               Cambridge, MA 02138
               Phone (866) 823-4726, Fax (617) 354-6875, E-mail info@hhpub.com
Europe: Hogrefe & Huber Publishers, Rohnsweg 25, D-37085 Göttingen, Germany,
               Phone +49 551 49609-0, Fax +49 551 49609-88, E-mail hh@hhpub.com

SALES & DISTRIBUTION
USA: Hogrefe & Huber Publishers, Customer Services Department,
               30 Amberwood Parkway, Ashland, OH 44805,
               Phone (800) 228-3749, Fax (419) 281-6883, E-mail custserv@hhpub.com
Europe: Hogrefe & Huber Publishers, Rohnsweg 25, D-37085 Göttingen, Germany,
               Phone +49 551 49609-0, Fax +49 551 49609-88, E-mail hh@hhpub.com

OTHER OFFICES
Canada: Hogrefe & Huber Publishers, 12 Bruce Park Avenue, Toronto, Ontario M4P 2S3
Switzerland: Hogrefe & Huber Publishers, Länggass-Strasse 76, CH-3000 Bern 9

Hogrefe & Huber Publishers
Incorporated and registered in the State of Washington, USA, and in Göttingen, Lower Saxony, Germany

Printed and bound in Germany
ISBN 0-88937-272-1

11/22/04

Contents

Foreword

The world is rapidly becoming a different place, and the challenges to individuals and societies imposed by globalization and modernization are widely acknowledged and apparent. Our increasingly diverse and interconnected populations, rapid technological change in the workplace and in everyday life, and the instantaneous availability of vast amounts of information represent but a few of these new demands. Other demands relate to the type of world OECD countries want to promote: balancing economic growth with the sustainability of natural environments, individual prosperity with social cohesion and reducing societal inequalities. The development of the knowledge, skills, and competencies of the population – through education systems and learning opportunities in the workplace and other venues through the life span – is key to meeting these demands. This necessarily sparks related questions about what are the competencies that are most important for today's and tomorrow's world and how they can be developed and fostered. OECD countries are at the forefront of addressing these issues and developing sound indicators of the knowledge and skills of young people and adults. To date, however, OECD work in this arena has focused on measuring individuals' reading, mathematical, and scientific literacy. The *Definition and Selection of Competencies: Theoretical and Conceptual Foundations* (DeSeCo) Project was initiated to provide solid theoretical and conceptual foundations for the broad range of competencies that are needed to face the challenges of the present and the future. The project, in which many OECD countries have participated, is led by the Swiss Federal Statistical Office in collaboration with the U.S. Department of Education, National Center for Education Statistics, and with support from Statistics Canada.

DeSeCo aimed to develop, through an interdisciplinary, collaborative, and forward-looking approach, a frame of reference for assessments and indicators of competencies that would have resonance with the information needs of policy-makers.

The first DeSeCo volume – *Defining and Selecting Key Competencies* – was published in 2001 and provides the scholarly contributions during the first phase of the project. In these papers, one can find the bases on which the DeSeCo framework is built and fully appreciate the rich interdisciplinary nature of the project. The present volume presents DeSeCo's final report. It is a vital contribution to advancing our understanding of what it means to be a competent individual and of how investments in key competencies can benefit both individuals and societies. DeSeCo's overarching framework is valuable because it provides a broad-based conceptual foundation that recognizes the complexity of the topic and stimulates us to take a more comprehensive view on why key competencies are important and to reflect on what we value in competent individuals and what type of world we are striving for.

DeSeCo's framework will serve as a guide to the OECD for the planning and implementation of a coherent, long-term strategy for assessments and indicators of key competencies among young people and adults. The DeSeCo framework could also find much wider application in the development of education and training programs for all stages of lifelong learning.

Many people made important contributions to the work of DeSeCo, but none more than Dominique Simone Rychen and Laura Salganik. Their commitment, their intellectual leadership, and their drive have ensured that the work has been brought to such a productive conclusion. Heinz

Gilomen and Eugene Owen provided the project with significant intellectual support and, through the Swiss Federal Statistical Office and the National Center for Education Statistics, with crucial financial support. I thank the four of them on behalf of all who enjoyed the opportunity to work with them on the project and all who will benefit from this publication.

Barry McGaw
Director for Education
OECD

Acknowledgments

We would like to express our sincere gratitude to those who have contributed immeasurably to the DeSeCo Project over the past five years. We are much indebted to Heinz Gilomen, Director of Social and Education Statistics at the Swiss Federal Statistical Office (SFSO) and chair of the DeSeCo Steering Group, whose leadership and intellectual input have been indispensable. Our thanks also go to the SFSO, its Director General, Adelheid Bürgi-Schmelz, and its former Director General, Carlo Malaguerra, for taking on the role of lead country for the project. We are very grateful to Barry McGaw, Director of the OECD's Directorate for Education; Andreas Schleicher, Head of the OECD's Indicators and Analysis Division; Eugene Owen, Director of the International Activities Program of the U.S. National Center for Education Statistics, (NCES); Valena White Plisko, Associate Commissioner of NCES; and T. Scott Murray, Director of Social and Institutional Statistics, Statistics Canada, for their support and participation as members of the DeSeCo Steering Group.

From its inception, this project has benefited from the interest and active participation of an international group of renowned scholars, experts, and policy-makers. We are grateful to the many individuals who contributed to the various activities throughout the project, including Jorma Ahola, Thomas Alexander, Marilyn Binkley, Norberto Bottani, Satya Brink, Martine Brunschwig Graf, Carlo Callieri, Monique Canto-Sperber, John Carson, Jacques Delors, Alexandra Draxler, Ruth Dreifuss, Rita Dunon, Jean-Pierre Dupuy, Jean-Claude Emin, Jean-Patrick Farrugia, Helmut Fend, Barbara Fratczak-Rudnicka, David Fretwell, Iddo Gal, Andrew Gonczi, Jack Goody, Marit Granheim, Tom Griffin, François Grin, Bob Harris, Helen Haste,

Thomas Healy, Hans Heijke, Willem Houtkoop, Walo Hutmacher, Daniel Keating, Robert Kegan, Frances Kelly, Eckhard Klieme, Erik Knain, Rainer Lehmann, Frank Levy, Denise Lievesley, Katharina Maag Merki, John Martin, John Morley, Urs Moser, Jay Moskowitz, Richard Murnane, Tim Oates, Attilio Oliva, Adama Ouane, Philippe Perrenoud, Jules Peschar, George Psacharopoulos, Reijo Raivola, Cecilia Ridgeway, Trevor Riordan, Laurell Ritchie, Gianni Rosas, Claude Sauvageot, Gerry Shiel, Jenny Soukkan, Sondra Stein, Erich Svecnik, Judith Torney-Purta, Uri Peter Trier, Albert Tuijnman, Leonardo Vanella, Peter Vogelius, Franz Weinert, Douglas Willms, and Ralf Witt.

We are particularly thankful to Jean-Pierre Dupuy, Helmut Fend, Jack Goody, Robert Kegan, Rolf Lischer, Heinz-Herbert Noll, Tim Oates, Philippe Perrenoud, Cecilia Ridgeway, Paul Röhtlisberger, and Uri Peter Trier for their valuable comments on drafts of the chapters in this book.

There are several individuals who were instrumental in preparing this book. We would particularly like to thank David Nohara and John Konstant for their invaluable writing and editorial assistance. We also extend our thanks to Caroline St. John-Brooks for her writing and editorial support. Last, many thanks to Andreas de Bruin of Publi Duty for the graphic design, Sanjay Seth for the layout, and Robin Gurley, Martin Hahn, Mary McLaughlin, and Marion Scotchmer of the Education Statistics Services Institute of the American Institutes for Research, for their help in preparing the final manuscript.

Introduction

A project defined

Recent trends toward increasing diversity and liberalization on the one hand, and continued globalization and standardization on the other hand, both within and across countries, present clear challenges. While individuals and the governments that represent them seek continuous economic growth, there is concern regarding the impact of this growth on natural and social environments (OECD, 2001d). In a similar vein, many are uneasy that although the rapid introduction of new technologies may increase productivity, it will also contribute to increasing social inequality. In such a context, education is widely considered an indispensable aspect of any and all conceptual and practical approaches to these issues, as evidenced by the ever-increasing emphasis that is placed on education as a resource and asset for individual and social achievement. With this heightened attention on education, tomorrow's curriculum has become a relevant topic for political discourse and education reform efforts all over the world. There is a growing concern among governments and the general public about the adequacy and quality of education and training, as well as the economic and social returns on public educational expenditures.

As a result, the Organisation for Economic Co-operation and Development (OECD) and other multinational institutions have invested considerable effort in the development of internationally comparable outcome indicators in the education field (Salganik, Rychen, Moser, & Konstant, 1999; Salganik, 2001). In general, these indicators measure traditional notions of academic achievement and skill development, such as reading and mathematics skills. This focus is partly the result of practical considerations, but is also due to the widely held and justifiable notion that these areas are crucial to success in the modern economy and society. Simultaneously, though, for some time it has been recognized that these curriculum-based and subject-related competencies and basic skills do not capture the full range of relevant education outcomes for human and social development and political and economic governance.

Apart from reading, writing, and computing, what other competencies are relevant for an individual to lead a successful and responsible life and for society to face the challenges of the present and the future? What are the normative, theoretical, and conceptual foundations for defining and selecting a limited set of individually based key competencies (Rychen, 2001)? An interest in such questions led to an international and interdisciplinary endeavor launched in late 1997 under the auspices of the OECD. This project, entitled *Definition and Selection of Competencies: Theoretical and Conceptual Foundations* (hereafter referred to as DeSeCo), has been carried out under the leadership of Switzerland.

DeSeCo's goal was the construction of a broad overarching conceptual frame of reference relevant to the development of individually based key competencies in a lifelong learning perspective, to the assessment of these competencies in an international setting, and to the development and interpretation of internationally comparable indicators. DeSeCo has considered the topic of important, necessary, or desirable competencies from a broad, holistic perspective. Thus, the reflection on key competencies was not limited to a particular context such as school and student achievement, or workers' skills and the demands of the labor market, or to what is easily or currently measurable in large-scale assessments. Rather, DeSeCo focused on competencies that contribute to a successful life and a well-functioning society.

Based on theoretical and conceptual approaches to competence and informed by political and practical considerations, the DeSeCo Project succeeded in developing a conceptual frame of reference for key competencies. The present volume delineates this framework whereby demand-oriented competencies are conceptualized within a three-fold categorization. The DeSeCo framework provides a solid conceptual underpinning for future international efforts to assess the competencies of young people and adults within, and possibly beyond, the OECD. The results also present a reference point for interpreting empirical findings about the outcomes of learning and teaching. Further, this volume offers an important contribution to the debate on priority areas for competence development and on policies aimed at enhancing key competencies for all. What follows in this introduction is an outline of the basic considerations underlying the DeSeCo Project and a description of the processes that contributed to the results.

Basic considerations and research questions

DeSeCo originated in a governmental context, the OECD, and thus is organized as a policy-driven research project. The following questions exemplify the issues that have guided the reflections and conceptual work on key competencies (Rychen & Salganik, 2001):

- Can a set of competencies of prime importance for a successful life and effective participation in different fields of life – including economic, political, social, and family domains; public and private interpersonal relations; and individual personal development – be identified?

- If so, what is the nature of these competencies and what distinguishes them as key competencies? How can they be described and theoretically justified? What are the components of these competencies? Is the premise of a limited number of key competencies justified?

- Do key competencies operate independently, or should they be viewed as an interdependent set or constellation of competencies?

- To what extent are key competencies immutable with reference to social, economic, and cultural conditions? To what extent are they generally valid from country to country or from region to region?

- To what extent is it possible to identify key competencies independently of age, gender, status, professional activity, etc? Are certain competencies particularly important in the various phases of life and, if so, which ones? Do we need the same key competencies when we are young, join the workforce, establish a family, advance in our professional or political careers, or retire?

- What are the consequences of these results for the development and interpretation of indicators?

From the start of this study, it was clear that determining key competencies is not simply an academic exercise. As one contributor to DeSeCo wrote, "It is not enough for experts simply to define a conceptual and methodological framework. The question is both ethical and political" (Perrenoud,

2001, p. 121). Ultimately, the identification of a valuable and legitimate set of key competencies is the result of a process of analysis and discussion that occurs in the realm of policy and politics, in which academics are only one of several stakeholders. To this end, the DeSeCo Project has attempted to broaden the discussion by inviting participation from a variety of experts and policy-makers representing the range of interested parties.

Several notions have been emphasized throughout the project as particularly relevant to the topic of key competencies. First, DeSeCo does not deal with competencies simply from the point of view of society's basic functioning and individuals' immediate survival. It approaches the question of competencies via the perspective of a successful life and a well-functioning society, conceiving the potential societal benefits of a well-educated citizenry as including a productive economy, democratic processes, social cohesion, and peace. At the individual level, the potential benefits of competencies entail successful participation in the labor market, in political processes, and in social networks; and meaningful interpersonal relations and general satisfaction with one's life.

Second, although cognitive skills and knowledge – as explicitly transmitted through traditional school programs – are important education outcomes, the reflection on competencies cannot be limited to such elements. Both labor market behavior and current research on intelligence and learning indicate the importance of noncognitive factors such as attitudes, motivation, and values, which are not necessarily or exclusively acquired and developed in the domain of formal education.

Third, terms such as *key* or *core competencies*, *life skills*, or *basic skills* are in widespread use with multiple, varied, and ambiguous definitions. Therefore, a clarification of the concept of competence and related terms is indispensable.

Finally, DeSeCo recognizes that multiple approaches to the notion of key competence exist. Depending on the perspective, different and not necessarily compatible arguments and methodologies may be emphasized. Thus, competencies need to be examined from multiple disciplinary and practical viewpoints.

In light of these basic considerations, constructing a solid overarching frame of reference required the project to focus on the theoretical constructs and models that underlie and guide analyses and discussions on key competencies, to explicitly include the normative considerations inherent to the undertaking, and, last but not least, to consider the definition and selection processes that take place in different socioeconomic and cultural environments. The project's work program, in turn, was designed to fulfill these criteria to the widest extent possible.

The work program

DeSeCo's work program was designed to include multiple perspectives on the topic of competencies and to encourage dialogue and exchange among various stakeholders at the national and international levels. The work program consisted of four major activities.

The first activity was a critical analysis of several studies conducted during the 1990s in OECD countries related to indicators of education outcomes (Salganik et al., 1999). The analysis focused on the origin of concepts, the theoretical and normative considerations, and the mechanisms of the definition processes that influenced the conceptualization and realization of the studies in question.

Building a common understanding depends to a great deal on common language and meaningful terms; otherwise, one risks juggling with catchwords only. In light of the terminological and conceptual confusion related to notions such as competence, skills, qualifications, standards, literacy, and so on, the second major activity was a preliminary clarification of the concept of competence (Weinert, 2001).

The third activity of DeSeCo's work program was the determination of theory-grounded sets of key competencies through the input of expert opinions. Scholars[1] from different academic disciplines (anthropology, economics, philosophy, psychology, and sociology) were each asked to construct a set of relevant key competencies from their own theoretical background and disciplinary perspective. They were expected to justify their selections theoretically, taking into account any available state-of-the-art research-based evidence. Subsequently, a commenting process was initiated, wherein the scholarly papers were distributed among the authors, other academics, and leading representatives from various fields.[2] It was a first step to exploring the main convergences and divergences among the different disciplinary perspectives and to gain insight into priority areas from a more practical and policy-oriented perspective.

Finally, a country consultation process (CCP) was organized within the OECD to review national experiences in the definition and selection of key competencies and issues related to the development and assessment of competencies (Trier, 2003). Twelve countries[3] prepared national reports on the topic of key competencies and education indicators. The result was a clarification of the various approaches taken by different countries to determine and satisfy national education needs and priorities.

---

[1] The scholars are Monique Canto-Sperber, Centre National de la Recherche Scientifique, France, and Jean-Pierre Dupuy, Ecole Polytechnique, Centre de Recherche en Epistémologie Appliquée, France, representing a philosophical perspective; Jack Goody, St. John's College, University of Cambridge, United Kingdom, representing an anthropological perspective; Helen Haste, University of Bath, United Kingdom, representing a psychological perspective; Frank Levy, Massachusetts Institute of Technology, United States, and Richard J. Murnane, Harvard University, United States, representing an economic perspective; and Philippe Perrenoud, University of Geneva, Switzerland, representing a sociological perspective. Their contributions are published in Rychen and Salganik (2001).

[2] The commentators included Carlo Callieri, Confindustria, Italy; Jacques Delors and Alexandra Draxler, Task Force on Education for the Twenty-first Century, UNESCO; Jean-Patrick Farrugia, Le Mouvement des Entreprises de France (MEDEF), France; Bob Harris, Education International; Robert Kegan, Harvard University, United States; George Psacharopoulos, University of Athens, Greece (formerly with the World Bank); Cecilia Ridgeway, Stanford University, United States; Laurell Ritchie, Canadian Auto Workers, Canada; M. Boediono, Ministry of Education and Culture, Indonesia; and Leonardo Vanella, Centro de Estudios e Investigación del Desarrollo Infanto-Juvenil, Argentina. Most of these comments are published in Rychen and Salganik (2001).

[3] Austria, Belgium (Flanders), Denmark, Finland, France, Germany, the Netherlands, New Zealand, Norway, Sweden, Switzerland, and the United States.

Debates and exchange: From multiple perspectives toward interdisciplinary insight

Each of the four activities described above highlighted the specific challenges that DeSeCo would have to overcome and reinforced the project's
intention to bring together the knowledge and insight gained from these
activities. To that end, a series of events was organized to move from specific activities and multiple perspectives toward a common understanding
of the issues at stake and, eventually, to a consensus on an integrated frame
of reference.

DeSeCo Symposium 1999

The first international symposium,[4] held in Neuchâtel, Switzerland, in
October 1999, was a forum for intense debate and exchange among about
60 invited experts and academics. It brought together the authors of the
scholarly papers representing the different disciplinary perspectives, other
academics, and representatives of leading social and economic institutions
to reflect on DeSeCo's aforementioned first three activities. The symposium
succeeded in

- creating an international network of academics and experts representing different disciplines and social fields interested in collaborat-
  ing and working together toward an overarching conceptual framework for identifying key competencies,

- increasing the discussion and awareness of the issues inherent in dealing with questions of competencies and their assessment, and

- clarifying which avenues would be particularly fruitful for further
  work in this area.

Expert papers prepared in conjunction with the first DeSeCo symposium
were compiled into *Defining and Selecting Key Competencies*, released in
August 2001 (Rychen & Salganik, 2001).

---

[4] For information about this symposium, go to
http://www.statistik.admin.ch/stat_ch/ber15/deseco/deseco_symp99.htm

Following the symposium, the conceptual work on key competencies progressed as two subsequent workshops with the authors of the scholarly papers were organized to further explore possible commonalities and differences in defining and selecting key competencies. In light of these reflections, an interim synthesis (Rychen & Salganik, 2000) was prepared laying out DeSeCo's findings on a number of theoretical and conceptual issues and outlining common features among the proposed approaches to defining and selecting competencies.

Toward a consolidation of the overarching frame of reference

During 2001, a number of additional expert papers were commissioned to complement and extend the examination of key competencies represented in the first publication.[5] Based on the expert papers contributed throughout the project and the country reports, a revised synthesis in the form of a discussion paper was prepared in anticipation of a second international symposium (Rychen & Salganik, 2002). The discussion paper outlined the major themes and theses developed in the course of DeSeCo's work program. Rather than focus on the extraordinary richness and diversity found

---

[5] The authors included Barbara Fratczak-Rudnicka, Warsaw University, Poland; Judith Torney-Purta, University of Maryland, United States; Daniel Keating, University of Toronto, Canada; and Tim Oates, Qualifications and Curriculum Authority, London, United Kingdom. These papers are published in Rychen, Salganik, and McLaughlin (2003).

in the contributions (which could not have been presented adequately), it focused on the common strands as a means of moving toward a consensus about key competencies for the 21st century.

DeSeCo Symposium 2002

A second international DeSeCo symposium was held in February 2002 in Geneva.[6] The symposium provided further opportunity to work toward a consensus on key competencies among a wide range of countries, stakeholders, and interest groups. The various inputs and the engaging discourses of the various sessions at the symposium enabled the project to take an important step toward a more coherent view of what constitutes key competencies.

DeSeCo's final conclusions and recommendations

In response to an OECD request, a strategy paper with the project's conclusions and recommendations was prepared during the first half of 2002 (OECD, 2002). The strategy paper is further developed in this volume, the final report of the DeSeCo Project, which draws primarily on contributions to DeSeCo since its inception.

As described in this introduction, DeSeCo's conclusions and recommendations are the ultimate result of an international collaborative effort among scholars from different disciplines; experts from education, business, labor, health, and other relevant sectors; specialists in large-scale assessments; and representatives of OECD member countries and of international

---

[6] For more information about this symposium, go to
   http://www.statistik.admin.ch/stat_ch/ber15/deseco_int02.htm

organizations such as UNESCO, the World Bank, the International Labour Organisation (ILO), and the United Nations Development Program (UNDP).

Outline of this volume

In chapter 1, Laura Hersh Salganik and Maria Stephens provide a backdrop for the subsequent chapters with an analysis of contributions to DeSeCo from the policy sector, including the country reports from the CCP.

Chapters 2, 3, and 4 delineate the major theoretical and conceptual elements of DeSeCo's overarching frame of reference for key competencies. Chapter 2, by Dominique Simone Rychen and Laura Hersh Salganik, presents a holistic model of competence, which integrates and relates demands, cognitive and noncognitive prerequisites, and context into a complex action system. Chapter 3, by Dominique Simone Rychen, lays out analytical criteria for defining and selecting key competencies leading to a three-fold categorization for key competencies – interacting in socially heterogeneous groups, acting autonomously, and using tools interactively. In chapter 4, Heinz Gilomen addresses the topic of conceptual linkages between key competencies and the quality of a successful life and a well-functioning society and, as an initial step, outlines a number of critical dimensions of these desired outcomes.

Chapters 5 and 6 move the discussion to the realm of assessments and indicators of key competencies. Chapter 5, by T. Scott Murray, discusses the broad policy relevance of assessments of key competencies and the implications of DeSeCo's frame of reference for the development of assessments and indicators in the future. In chapter 6, Andreas Schleicher, writing from an OECD perspective, discusses the challenges associated with the development of a coherent, long-term assessment strategy based on the theoretical and conceptual foundations provided by DeSeCo.

The book closes with concluding remarks by Heinz Gilomen and an afterword by Eugene H. Owen.

Chapter 1

Competence priorities in policy and practice

Laura Hersh Salganik and Maria Stephens

Introduction

The purpose of this chapter is to describe the various ways that key competencies have been thought about and addressed in OECD countries. It provides an analysis of the approaches taken to defining and selecting key competencies and, in doing so, identifies some of the differences across and within countries. By exploring the multiple activities associated with key competencies, both in the policy realm and in practice and in different social spheres or contexts, this chapter will also set a backdrop for the conceptualization of key competencies within the DeSeCo Project.

The chapter draws primarily on comments from policy-makers and experts in economic and social fields contributed at different phases of the project and reports from a country contribution process (CCP) conducted within DeSeCo. The CCP, in which OECD member countries were invited to participate, aimed to solicit and introduce national views on competencies to the process of defining and selecting key competencies[1] and to supplement the theoretical work being undertaken simultaneously. Twelve countries[2] participated in the CCP and submitted reports, which were synthesized by Uri Peter Trier (2003) in his summary report.[3]

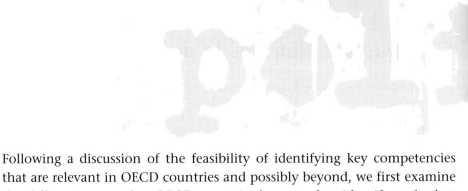

Following a discussion of the feasibility of identifying key competencies that are relevant in OECD countries and possibly beyond, we first examine the different approaches OECD countries have used to identify and select key competencies, that is, the *activities* through which discussions and applications of competencies manifest themselves. We then discuss the resulting *content*, namely, similarities and differences among the competencies they identify. In many cases, the approaches vary by sector (e.g., education, the economy) as well as by country. However, as Trier (2003) points out, there are many significant similarities with respect to content that transcend the multiple approaches.[4]

---

[1] A variety of terms are used in the CCP reports, such as essential or core competencies or skills. These terms are used interchangeably throughout this chapter.

[2] The twelve countries were Austria, Belgium (Flanders), Denmark, Finland, France, Germany, the Netherlands, New Zealand, Norway, Sweden, Switzerland, and the United States. We also have drawn from other reports prepared for the DeSeCo Project, such as those from Australia (Gonczi, 2003), Canada (Brink, 2003), and England (Oates, 2003), which are not intended to be country-level reviews of activities related to competencies but rather descriptions of specific activities.

[3] The authors gratefully acknowledge this summary report (Trier, 2003) as an invaluable source in the preparation of this chapter and will credit many of the analyses and observations herein to it.

[4] In this and other sections, the descriptions of activities are based on commentaries and country reports solicited during and prior to 2000.

Insurmountable differences or common vision?

To start with, let us first raise the important question of whether it is possible to identify a set of competencies that can be considered key and have similar meanings across or even within OECD countries. Many DeSeCo commentators have rightly noted that competencies and the importance placed on them are related to differences in culture, context, and values. This issue was raised frequently as a challenge for working toward a common set of key competencies.

The interpretation of autonomy as a widely held value provides an excellent example. As the New Zealand report (Kelly, 2001) points out, the idea that autonomous and reflective behavior by individuals is a desirable characteristic reflects a Western paradigm, aspects of which can often be in conflict with Mäori and Pacific peoples' cultures, which emphasize consensus decision-making, collective responsibilities, and group competencies. Tim Oates (2003) offers another example, citing the differences in how capitalist societies and middle-Asian communal economies might view "respect for property" and how that, in turn, would affect the value placed on competencies related to it. Thus, the roles of individuals within society and the balance between individual and collective competencies can be an important cultural difference.

Even in cases where a common value or competence area is identified, such as communication or citizenship, the particulars of the competencies comprising it and how they would be evaluated differ across communities. For instance, how is the ability to communicate considered when different groups use different forms of communication with different rules of etiquette? Do the competencies required to be a "good citizen" differ across countries (Fratczak-Rudnicka & Torney-Purta, 2003)? It is concerns such as these that led to the suggestion from French authorities to focus on specific populations (e.g., the underskilled) within specific contexts in individual countries' training and work systems rather than work toward international comparisons of universal competencies (Emin, 2003).

Cultural differences are obvious, as are their implications for the development of empirical comparisons of competencies across countries. However, as stated in Trier's (2003) summary report:

> *Nobody who supports the idea of universal key competencies is suggesting that these competencies could not or should not be related to concrete social and cultural contexts. And almost nobody who believes that competencies cannot be sensibly discussed without relating them to specific contexts and socio-political conditions will deny the existence of universal values.* (section 6.5)

This statement complements Franz E. Weinert (2001), who emphasizes that activities to identify a common set of key competencies can be fruitful as long as they are placed within a normative framework that acknowledges and incorporates such differences.

Jacques Delors and Alexandra Draxler (2001) point out that as we constantly recognize the importance of context and cultural differences, it is important to also keep in mind that there are things that we share. The evidence for Delors and Draxler of the possibility of developing and working from a common vision is the very fact that we routinely undertake major collective endeavors – consider the establishment of the United Nations and its various missions and activities – that rely on the belief that there are some ideals we have in common. They also draw on the specific example of the International Commission on Education for the 21st Century, which is much related to the DeSeCo Project's purposes and which discovered a striking agreement among countries about the nature of important competencies (e.g., making and applying moral judgments, describing the world and our own real and desirable place in it, marshaling our own skills to construct a future that involves living in society) (UNESCO, 1996). While they recognize that people or governments may not universally practice such common ideals, they counter that it cannot be argued that these ideals do not exist. To them, many of the differences observed across countries reflect a "diversity of application," not of aspiration (Delors & Draxler, p. 215).

Key competencies in education, the economy, and other sectors

The concept of key competence has been relevant for policy discussions in different social fields in many OECD countries. However, while the different sectors often are reacting to the same broad demands imposed by rapid technological advances, globalization, and a subsequent movement toward developing knowledge economies, their specific needs for and approaches to identifying key competencies are somewhat, and perhaps understandably, different. Such a sector-based distinction emerges in most of the reports from the CCP, as well as in other sources.

For instance, in education, key competencies often are associated with the broadening of general and vocational education and also with reforming education for social renewal. In the economy, key competencies are associated with new forms of business and job organization, although nuances emerge as multiple perspectives within the economic sector (e.g., business, industry, labor) are explored. Reports from representatives of civic society emphasize in particular the importance of achieving societal balance and fostering active democratic participation.

Key competencies in the education sector

Certainly, it comes as no surprise that education is one of the sectors of society in which the notion of competencies and their development has been and still is being addressed and debated. In nearly all the CCP reports, competencies were discussed extensively from this perspective.

Within the education sector, competencies are approached in several ways that are generally related to curricular reform and the expansion or refinement of educational objectives. From the CCP and other sources, competencies have appeared in (1) requirements for the completion of upper secondary school, (2) school curricula, and (3) all-encompassing educational goals.

School leaving requirements

In at least two countries, Germany and Switzerland, competencies that span subject areas have been embedded in the requirements for achieving the academic upper secondary school leaving certificate – the *Abitur* in the former and the *Maturität* in the latter. For instance, earning the *Abitur* requires that in addition to achievement in traditional subjects such as German language, foreign language, and mathematics, students acquire 12 overarching competencies, including understanding the structure of knowledge, directing one's own learning, reflecting on one's own learning, and thinking, judging, and acting (Witt & Lehmann, 2001). Switzerland's "transdisciplinary goals" for the *Maturität* identify 12 similar competencies, such as having the capacity for lifelong learning, the capacity for independent judgment, and intellectual openness (Trier, 2001b).

As Trier (2003) points out, the motivation in these countries for the explicit inclusion of these broad competence requirements goes as far back as the 1960s, to perceived deficiencies in the existing education system and to the application of educational research findings, which promoted educational reform through the establishment of more integrated curricula. Establishing broad competence requirements has thus been seen as a means to foster and achieve integrated curricula, improvements in schooling, and greater equity among students. Trier also notes, however, that historically there has been a gap between stated goals and actual practice, although in the future such competencies may become fully integrated into the practice of existing systems, as external pressure on school systems regarding their importance increases.

School curricula

In some other countries, competencies find a no less important place in newly revised or developed curriculum documents. One example is in Austria, where perceived social and technological changes resulted in pressure for change in the education system. The term *key skills* was associated with criticism of an overemphasis on knowledge in general education and specialization in vocational education (Lassnigg, Mayer, & Svecnik, 2001). In 1999, Austria reformed its curriculum for students ages 10 to 14 in order to expand its existing focus on subject-matter knowledge to include more "personality-driven" competencies and those that reinforce a "real-life orientation" (Lassnigg et al.). Five educational areas were defined to encourage the integration of disciplines and the new competencies: language and communication, mankind and society, nature and technology, creativity and design, and health and exercise. In this way, it is somewhat similar to the previous examples, in that competencies become vehicles to encourage organizational models that reinforce or advance desired educational reforms.

This also was the case with a project in Flemish Belgium, in which a consortium of middle schools developed a reference framework for key competencies for the basic curriculum for 12- to 14-year-old students. The approach views human beings as "a crossroads of relationships" (Dunon, 2001, p. 4) and identifies five broad competencies that are important for participating in a critical and creative way in the development of society and of oneself. What is interesting is that this consortium also views the debates and activities surrounding key competencies as an opportunity to accelerate desired reforms in school culture and teaching practice.

A final example involves curriculum in vocational education. In Germany, the approach has been to use a small number of competence areas –

domain-related, personal, and social competence – as a guide for organizing curriculum into thematic units (Witt & Lehmann, 2001; Oates, 2003). This contrasts with the approach in England, where during the 1990s, considerable effort was devoted to identifying key skills to enable workers to cope with increasing complexity in work tasks. From very early on, the effort was characterized by a desire to assess students in the skill areas (Oates). Thus, the key skills identified – which are grouped into six broad areas (communications, application of number, information technology, working with others, improving one's own learning and performance, and problem-solving) – are further specified at five levels of performance. Oates suggests that the assessment-driven nature of the use of key skills in England makes it fundamentally different from activities that are driven by a pedagogical focus.

All-encompassing educational goals

Competencies also have earned a place in the overall educational goals in several countries, namely, the Nordic countries, Germany, and New Zealand. In Norway and New Zealand, for example, comprehensive curriculum statements that focus on the whole education system[5] demonstrate a broad view of the purpose of education and include many overarching competencies. Norway's curriculum describes its goal as one of developing "integrated human beings," individuals who are spiritual, creative, working, liberally educated, social, and environmentally aware (Knain, 2001). New Zealand, following a 1988 document outlining four broad goals of education, specified eight essential skills that students should possess: communication skills, numeracy skills, information skills, problem-solving skills, self-management and competitive skills, social and cooperative skills, physical skills, and work and study skills (Kelly, 2001).

Both Sweden and Finland identify competence areas of a more general nature that should be developed and assessed in schools. In Sweden, these include seeing connections and being able to find one's way in the outside world, making conscious ethical decisions, understanding and applying

---

[5] Norway's Core Curriculum includes primary, secondary, and adult education. New Zealand's Curriculum Framework covers students through upper secondary school.

democracy, and being creative and able to communicate (Skolverket, 2001). In Finland, they include learning to learn, communication competencies, and lifelong learning, with component competencies further identified under these headings (Etelälahti & Sahi, 2001). In Denmark, where competencies are taking a prominent place in industrial development policy, they appear in education through the various national decrees that govern the different levels of education (e.g., primary, secondary, vocational, adult) and that emphasize education's purpose to foster "active participation in a democratic society" and "personal development" (Otterstrom, 2001). In Germany, the *Forum Bildung* (Education Forum), an initiative of the Federal Minister of Education and Research and the *Länder*-based Ministers of Education, released preliminary guidelines for articulating educational aims, which recognize the importance of individual development and social participation as aims of both general and vocational education. The guidelines propose six fundamental competencies: intelligent knowledge, applicable knowledge, learning competence, method-related/instrumental key competencies, social competencies, and value orientation (Witt & Lehmann, 2001).

The impetus for developments in the countries discussed in this section is a broader national effort for societal renewal, to which education is an essential contributor (Trier, 2003). Whereas in some of the previous examples relating to school-leaving requirements and curricula, the driving question was "How can education be improved?", here the question seems to have been "What can education do and what is it for?" – with the answer being that education should be more holistic, achieving broad humanistic goals.

In contrast, in the United States, concerns that the graduates of the education system would not have the skills to keep the country economically competitive culminated in the publication of *A Nation at Risk* (National Commission on Excellence in Education, 1983) and set the context for discussions on competencies. Thus, discussions on competencies in the United States at the national level took the form of setting standards and maintaining competitiveness (Trier, 2001c, 2003).

In the foregoing analysis, the groupings reflect the subtle differences in the approaches being taken across countries toward competencies, even within a single sector. Cutting across these examples, we draw on Trier's (2003) observation of the evolution of competencies in goals and curricula in OECD countries more generally. He reminds us how, at first, these competencies might have been woven into, or implicit in, programs of study, but how over time they emerged more explicitly in goals and frameworks or in targeted areas. Finally, in the last decade, competencies have appeared in curriculum documents with indications of which ones are of particular importance for education systems to develop. In each of these cases, key competencies have provided a perspective that either complements or provides an alternative to the traditional use of subject matter as the primary schema for organizing learning in schools.

Key competencies in the economic sector

The notion of competencies, and in particular key competencies, is also the focus of a great deal of attention, discussion, and effort in the economic sector, from both employers and employees. In the economic sector, educational outcomes are seen as crucial factors for productivity and competitiveness. The importance of worker quality, skills, and competencies as key for survival and "the first strategic factor that can be used to boost productivity and market competitiveness" (Callieri, 2001, p. 228) was underscored by various commentators from the business perspective (see also Farrugia, 2001; Oliva, 2003).

The discussion in the economic sector on key competencies is directed both outwardly – to education and training systems regarding their role in developing competencies – and inwardly – to its own communities, employers who want to attract and manage competent employees, and employees (e.g., unions) who want to identify and gain access to opportunities to develop key competencies. Activities related to competencies in the economic sector have included (1) competence or skill development and management as a new employer strategy, (2) labor union concerns and initiatives, (3) occupational profiles and job analyses, and (4) employer surveys of key competencies.

In contrast to the examples from the education sector, the activities that are described in this section do not focus on identifying key competencies, which are not typically the subject of much debate. As Attilio Oliva (2003) explains: "There are certain areas in which there is a growing agreement on what are considered 'key competencies,' specifically in the world of work and business... The more the pattern of the market with its rules extends, the more common and evident are the key competencies required to perform in it successfully" (section 2). Rather, in the economic sector, most of the examples relate to acquiring, evaluating, or managing key competencies.

Competence development and management as an employer strategy

Discussions on competencies arise in the economic sector from an organizational perspective, namely, from the increasing regard given to the importance of the development and management of competencies. Broadly speaking, this refers to treating competencies and their development as integral components of organizational decisions regarding staffing and training, within the overarching goal of organizational management and improvement.

For employers, the focus is on competence as a guiding framework for career development and human resource management. In France, this reflects a fairly major shift in attitudes among employers whereby they view their employees' careers in terms of a competence-building process and look for ways to use the notion of competencies to supplement – or even replace – the use of qualifications (e.g., years of experience, education) to develop and manage human resources. Competence development and management, furthermore, is viewed as a tool that will better ensure that employees are able to respond to new and changing situations in the workplace (Farrugia, 2001; Ministère de l'Education Nationale, 2001). For example, the *Mouvement des Entreprises de France* (MEDEF) is an initiative representing employers in France aimed at exploring the new social relationships between employers and workers being brought about by the importance of the development of skills and competencies to businesses' survival (Farrugia). MEDEF identifies competence management as a key strategy in creating conditions for productivity. In MEDEF's estimation, workers are responsible for upgrading their skills in order to remain in the "employability circle," whereas employers are responsible for the provision of resources for competence development and for organizing production in ways that will make the best use of workers' competencies.

The report from Flemish Belgium also notes that competence management is becoming a "key component in the structure and strategy of an increasing number of organizations" (Dunon, 2001, p. 5). In many Flemish companies, competence development and management is beginning to be used to recruit, train, and select employees and is closely tied to the specific goals of the respective companies. Although the interest in competence management comes mainly from a human capital development perspective, the Flemish report also notes an awareness that competence management can play a role in empowering employees for independent and autonomous learning.

Hand in hand with competence development and management from the career management perspective, at least theoretically, are the activities in some countries to establish systems to better or more comprehensively recognize individuals' competencies. Again, we draw on examples from France and Flemish Belgium.

Several recent legislative and institutional provisions in France have attempted to make possible the evaluation of a broad range of competencies in order to address the critical question of how "all citizens can gain recognition for the job skills acquired outside of formal training" (see, Ministère de l'Education Nationale, 2001, p. 5). The provisions are two-pronged. One prong is Skill Assessment Centers (the most recent version of a variety existing in France since the 1980s), which assist individuals in profiling their skills and competencies, researching and training for specific jobs, and becoming advocates in their own professional and competence development. The newest legislation relating to skills assessment allows employees to take leave from work to utilize these services. The second prong is the Validation of Job Experience provisions in two key pieces of legislation, which allow job experience to be substituted for other qualifications for entry into job training programs or to count toward a previously unearned diploma under certain guidelines.

In a similar vein, the offices of the ministers of education and employment in Flemish Belgium recently established a joint working group to develop an integrated model for the recognition of competencies (Dunon, 2001). Such a model would acknowledge those competencies gained in formal, semi-structured, and informal ways.

Labor union concerns and initiatives

From a labor perspective, however, there is a concern that competence development and management is fundamentally detrimental to workers, a tool to further control them and to erode the rights and protections they have gained through collective bargaining. Laurell Ritchie (2001) posits that employers promote competencies primarily in their own interests: "'Flexibility' is typically about market deregulation and the elimination of legislation and contract terms...employers can use 'teamwork' programs to set worker against worker with consequent job loss, and to build unquestioning conformity to a corporate culture" (p. 236). Moreover, Ritchie argues that employers use competence development and management as a means to shift the cost of training to workers. Rejecting the interpretation of human capital theory that states that individuals should invest in their own retraining, she comments, "This is a transparently self-serving interpretation on the part of those defending the corporate dumping of training costs" (p. 240). Ritchie's main critique is that the focus on competencies of workers shifts the balance of responsibility for unemployment and under-employment too far in the direction of the workers. She asks, "what if we turned this on its head?" (p. 237). For instance, flexibility would require that employers be flexible in accommodating workers' participation in education programs; trustworthiness would require that they observe "neutrality" during union organizing campaigns; teamwork would mean providing labor with equal participation in the introduction of new technologies and work methods.

Another major concern is that employers' focus on broad competencies will result in few opportunities for workers to develop new specific skills and qualifications that they believe will contribute more toward increasing their value in the labor market. This tension between broad and job-specific competencies (which labor views as a tension between rhetoric about the importance of broad competencies and the reality of the importance of job-specific skills) was frequently mentioned as a key issue to be taken into consideration in the debate on competencies in both the country reports (Trier, 2003) and other sources (Ritchie, 2001). More precisely, the tension reflects a concern among some actors (on both the labor and business sides) that focusing on general competencies could swing too far and ultimately lead to an overemphasis on personal qualities and a wholesale de-emphasis on context-specific vocational training. The implication is that the balance between general competencies, context- or job-specific competencies, and more traditional qualifications is a delicate one.

Labor unions themselves have been engaged in the identification of competencies, often as a first step in the broader goal of encouraging governmental and employer support for competence development. This is well described in a quote from the Austrian report:

> *Employee organizations have tried to make a contribution to the development of key competencies…by a range of different activities in respect of their own further education or the development of supportive teaching tools… As unionists, [they] were always the first to call for the conveyance of key skills…* (Lassnigg, 1998, as cited in Lassnigg et al., 2001, p. 22)

One of the countries to report at length about activities among unions was Sweden. In Sweden, the major trade unions (represented by the Swedish Trade Union Conference, the Swedish Confederation of Professional Employees, and the Swedish Confederation of Professional Associations) authored a joint memorandum in 2001 that was an attempt to develop a common framework for the discussion of issues related to lifelong learning and competence development. Their position supports the development of "the learning workplace," which they see as involving both personal and organizational-related development. The former captures, on the one hand, the idea that individuals have a responsibility for their own competence development but, on the other hand, that there also must be access to quality development opportunities. The latter reflects the idea that organizations also have a level of responsibility to identify which competencies are needed and to invest appropriately in their development in employees. The main idea of the memorandum was that competence development is an outlook, or an approach, to work and life that needs to be fostered not only at the individual level, but in supportive work environments as well (Skolverket, 2001).

The Swedish Metal Workers' Union takes this idea a step further, calling competence development and lifelong learning a human right. Its goal is to create the conditions for all workers to access learning opportunities that are clearly tied to their individual needs. In doing so, it describes competence as a four-pronged combination including "what one knows, what one can do, what one wants, and what one dares to do" (Skolverket, 2001, p. 10) and identifies a number of components at the organizational level that would promote competence development in order to help all individuals achieve their individual capacity (e.g., instituting work rotation systems, composing work teams with attention to members' individual competencies and interests, and fostering a positive regard for career development among managers).

Generally speaking, a major facet of unions' competence-related efforts is increasing workers' opportunities – especially among the most vulnerable (i.e., the lowest skilled) – for competence development. This is the case in the previous examples from Sweden and one from Denmark as well. The Danish Federation of Trade Unions, similar to the Swedish trade unions' joint activity, has been developing a strategy that focuses on the improvement of cooperation between employees and employers in order to increase employees' influence and responsibility at work and create more productive workplaces (Otterstrom, 2001). The messages coming out of this activity, however, are more similar to those expressed by the Swedish Metal Workers' Union, in that obtaining key competencies is viewed as a right and that employers should both provide opportunities for the development of new competencies and structure the work environment to allow workers to use what they have learned. An outgrowth of this activity is the union's attempt to monitor Denmark's competence, or human capital, to ensure that competence development is occurring not just for the elite but for the less educated worker as well (Danish Federation of Trade Unions, 1999).

Occupational profiles and job analyses

Activities in the economic sector to identify and define important competencies have taken the form, in several countries, of developing occupational profiles and conducting job analyses.

For example, in Flemish Belgium, the COBRA system is a catalog of required competencies for different careers in the Flemish labor market. What is most interesting is the recent agreement of the Flemish Employment Service and Vocational Training Agency, which is responsible for COBRA, to gear it in the future to the occupational profiles used by the Socio-Economic Council of Flanders. In other words, the training and economic sectors are forging a link around the shared importance of competencies. As a result of this collaboration and harmonization, the profiles also are now drawing out the most important tasks, knowledge, skills, and key competencies required by various professions or clusters of professions (Dunon, 2001).

The United States also has a nationally developed system to catalog and describe occupations and the skills and competencies that underlie them (Trier, 2001c, 2003). O*NET OnLine, from the U.S. Department of Labor, is a database and a tool that describes the skills required in different jobs at a fairly fine level of detail. For instance, while an overarching area is social skills, O*NET further breaks this down into components such as social perceptiveness, coordination, persuasion, and negotiation.

While the two preceding examples focus on the categorization and cataloging of competencies for use by employers, employees, and perhaps trainers, a final example under the job analysis heading – which, in fact, was a precursor to the O*NET example above – had a somewhat different purpose that involved a more inductive approach to identifying competencies. The Secretary's Commission on Achieving Necessary Skills (SCANS), appointed by the U.S. Secretary of Labor, drawing on analyses of 50 jobs and 900 underlying tasks, aimed to identify "workplace know-how." SCANS concluded with the identification of five competence areas (resources, interpersonal skills, information, systems, and technology) and three foundational areas (basic skills, thinking skills, and personal qualities) that are essential for those in the workforce to possess (U.S. Department of Labor, 1992, p. 83).

Employer surveys of key competencies

A final example of how the economic sector approaches competencies includes employer surveys, which attempt to identify the skills and competencies necessary for the workforce to acquire. For instance, recent surveys in New Zealand of employer expectations for entry-level job applicants showed that the vast majority of required competencies are interpersonal. The competencies frequently emphasized included communication, cooperation, creativity, and critical thinking, as well as the more traditional computational skills and computer literacy (Kelly, 2001). A survey of 709 employers in Finland identified 13 imperative competencies or qualities including, among others, initiative, interest, honesty, and conscientiousness (Etelälahti & Sahi, 2001). A study in Sweden further confirmed the importance employers attribute to broad competencies relative even to basic knowledge (Skolverket, 2001). And an international group of employer federations from seven European countries, in a statement to governments urging their support for improvements in education, stressed the importance of "emotional intelligence and control," identifying it as the most important competence when workers come together to collaborate (Oliva, 2003).

Key competencies in other contexts

Discussions of competencies have also been relevant in sectors other than education and the economy, though to a lesser extent and with less consistency across countries. From the country reports, we describe activities to identify key competencies in four other contexts: (1) indicators and assessments, (2) national-level research, (3) youth development, and (4) civic society.

Indicators and assessments

Several countries are engaged, either individually or collaboratively, in activities to develop indicators or to measure the competence levels of their populations. The activities may come out of labor ministries, education ministries, or collaborative efforts and may focus specifically on adult or student populations.

We first provide a few examples of indicator and assessment activities related mainly to adult populations. Denmark – through the Danish Economic Council, 53 affiliated companies, and other stakeholders in the public sector and academia – has established a National Competence Account, with the goal of monitoring Denmark's achievement of competencies for the knowledge society through the development of indicators. The National

Competence Account compares Denmark with six other OECD countries on 127 indicators, built around three identified core values (creativity, competitiveness, and cohesiveness) and competencies that fall under four main headings (learning, change, relationship, and meaning).

Several other countries are involved in activities to measure adult skills directly. For instance, France is planning a household survey of adults to collect data on their literacy and numeracy skills in contextualized situations, which planners believe is an essential element for obtaining valid information on adults' skills. In Canada, an extensive strategy for collecting data on skills has been developed in the broader context of its Skills Agenda in order to support human capital development, which is viewed as essential for improvements in innovation, productivity, and, ultimately, quality of life (Brink, 2003). The data strategy integrates across seven existing national and international surveys to cover the life span from birth to 90 years of age. Information about adults is drawn from four of these sources and includes both direct skills assessments and other contextual data.

There also are large-scale survey efforts to measure skills and competencies across countries. The Adult Literacy and Life Skills Survey (ALL) is being carried out in two waves, in 2003 and 2005, and assesses literacy, numeracy, and analytical reasoning skills. It also includes a survey on familiarity with information communication technology. ALL builds on the work of the International Adult Literacy Study, which was administered to adults in 20 countries in three waves during the mid- to late 1990s and which found important relationships between adults' literacy skills and their economic outcomes (see chapter 5). Most national and international assessments of school populations from the 1960s until 2000 focused on achievement in major school subject areas. More recently, however, studies have been conducted that aim to measure students' competencies more broadly. For example, the OECD's Programme for International Student Assessment (PISA) collects information on 15-year-old students' reading, mathematical, and scientific literacy, as well as on cross-curricular competencies (e.g., self-regulated learning and problem-solving). In another example, the IEA Civic Education Study measured the civic knowledge, skills, and attitudes of 14-year-old students.

National-level research activities

Two large-scale research projects of national scope were recently undertaken in Switzerland and the United States. The purpose of each of these projects was the identification (and, in the case of Switzerland, measurement) of comprehensive sets of key competencies and the preparation of related indicators. Although the methodological approaches taken differed, both projects realized empirically validated information on key competencies (Trier, 2003).

The Young Adult Survey in Switzerland aimed to measure how 18- to 20-year-olds performed on a variety of indicators of interdisciplinary objectives, or competencies. This research project began with an analysis of the goals of primary, secondary, and vocational curricula in Switzerland and the identification of a set of attainment targets, which were further tested, studied in regard to existing theoretical research, and refined into a set of 15 constructs that could be considered indicative of important key competencies (Grob & Maag Merki, 2001).

In the United States, Equipped for the Future: What Adults Need to Know and Be Able to Do in the 21st Century (EFF) aimed to identify which competencies mattered most to adults in fulfilling the sixth National Education Goal, which was for "every adult American to be literate and possess the knowledge and skills necessary to compete in the global economy and exercise the rights and responsibilities of citizenship" (National Education Goals Panel, 1999).[6] The approach was to analyze, based on survey and focus group responses, what activities adults thought they needed most in their different roles as citizens, family members, and workers and to identify which skills underlay those activities (Merrifield, 2000). In the end, 16 EFF Standards, called "generative skills," were established, along with 13 common activities. EFF was an important source for the identification of key competencies in DeSeCo's three-fold categorization of key competencies (see chapter 3).

---

[6] The National Education Goals Panel was established in 1990 as an independent executive branch agency of the federal government charged with monitoring national and state progress toward the National Education Goals, which had been agreed to by state governors and the President in 1989. The panel functioned until early 2002, when it was dissolved pursuant to the enactment of the new education law in the United States.

Though arguably the sets of competencies identified by each project have some similarities in content (e.g., cooperation is on both lists), Trier (2003) notes how the differing methodologies affect "profoundly the categories and the form in which the competencies are aggregated to construct 'key competencies'" (section 2.2). In the Swiss case, the constructs are generally overarching and have their roots in the theories and pedagogical goals of the country. In the U.S. case, the skills are more specifically described and have their roots in what are perceived to be common demands.

A youth development perspective

Discussions on competencies also arise in initiatives outside the formal education system that aim to contribute to the social, emotional, physical, and/or intellectual development of young people. Projects undertaken in this context often underline the importance of family and community support in the development of key competencies. In the United States, a research project to conceptualize the life skills necessary for young people's development was conducted by the 4-H (Hands, Health, Head, Heart) program. The program is affiliated with the U.S. Department of Agriculture and has been running nonformal education activities for young people 5 to 19 years old since 1914. The skills identified are organized around the four "H"s: Hands (giving, working), Health (being, living), Head (thinking, managing), and Heart (relating, caring) (Trier, 2001c). In the Netherlands, the Council for Youth Policy identified a set of six key competencies that are necessary for young people to cope with the demands and challenges they face (Peschar, 2001). These included self-steering, self-confidence, communication, problem-solving, engagement, and commitment.

A civic society perspective

Representatives of civic society tend to discuss competencies not so much in terms of lists of needed or important skills and qualities, but rather in terms of selected activities such as voting or participating in community activities, which are seen as contributing to desired social goals (e.g., balance, equity, cohesiveness, active democracy). The tone of the discourse on competencies in the civic sphere is generally one of perceived or potential deficiencies in these activities. Reports from studies in at least two countries suggest that the competencies for political participation may be lacking among the population (Trier, 2001b, on Switzerland; National Commission on Civic Renewal, 1998, on the United States). Results from the IEA Civic Education Study, which assessed 14-year-old students in 28 OECD and other countries, were somewhat more optimistic (Torney-Purta, Lehmann, Oswald, & Schulz, 2001).

The civic society perspective also reminds us, as other examples have, that competencies are found (or demonstrated) not just at an individual level, but at the societal level as well. This is exemplified by the model of the IEA study, which viewed civic competencies as relating to the ways in which individuals become increasingly connected to communities at the personal, local, national, and international levels, and the processes of civic learning that involve the growth of meaning-making, practice, relation to community, and formation of identity (Fratczak-Rudnicka & Torney-Purta, 2003).

Lists of key competencies

The preceding section focused on different activities that resulted in the identification of key competencies. This section brings us back to what came out of those activities at the level of content – that is, which key competencies were identified – and addresses the question of whether we can draw any, even preliminary, conclusions about key competencies across sectors and countries.

Priority areas across sectors and countries

The CCP reports and other sources include many different sets or lists of key competencies. Despite national differences and specificities in the sectors considered, we can highlight some important and compelling commonalities, thus providing evidence that it may be possible to construct key competencies that will be valued and applicable across sectors and nations.

Convergence across sectors

An easy conclusion to draw from the preceding section would be that there is a divergence in the discussion of key competencies between the education and economic (and other) sectors. While this might be partly true, a closer look at the content of the discussions shows that the convergence between the sectors is actually larger than the divergence (Trier, 2003).

First, the differences between sectors often actually stem from differences in semantics. For example, in the education sector, key competencies are in many cases identified in the context of specifying goals for education, curriculum development, or learning standards – without direct or explicit reference to key competencies. This is in contrast to the economic sector, where key competencies often are referred to more directly, albeit with a variety of terms.

Second, the main differences between sectors do not come from the identification of which key competencies matter but from the relative importance given to them or their component parts. For example, a "value orientation" competence area merits considerable discussion in both the education and economic sectors. However, the education sector tends to emphasize ethics, social and democratic values, tolerance, and human rights, whereas the economic sector tends to emphasize personal virtues such as integrity, reliability, loyalty, and honesty (Trier, 2003). This is not to say that integrity is not important to education or that tolerance is not important in the workplace, simply that different strands of the same general idea may be relatively more (or less) important in one sector than in another because of its particular focus, needs, and purposes.

Common competence areas across countries

The CCP reports showed that similar competencies, or competence areas with almost identical content, are held in common and emphasized as being particularly important across the participating countries. The aggregation of frequently mentioned competence areas proposed in the CCP summary report offers a valuable list of areas of particular interest and relevance in a number of OECD countries (table 1).

High	Medium	Low
Social competencies/ cooperation	Self-competence/self-management	Health/sports/physical competence
Literacies/intelligent and applicable knowledge	Political competence/ democracy	Cultural competencies (aesthetic, creative, intercultural, media)
Learning competencies/ lifelong learning	Ecological competence/ relation to nature	
Communication competencies	Value orientation	

Table 1: Frequency of mentions of key competence areas in country reports
Source: Trier (2003, section 2.3.3)

Virtually all participating countries recognize the importance of areas related to social competencies/cooperation, literacies/intelligent and applicable knowledge, learning, and communication. To define these competence areas, we draw virtually verbatim from Trier (2003):

• Social competencies and cooperation consist of interpersonal skills such as cooperation with others, advocating and influencing, and resolving conflict and negotiating. In a narrower sense, this competence area addresses working together, guiding and supporting others, seeking guidance and support from others, and (crucially) understanding and cooperating with people from different cultural backgrounds. However, this competence area is one that is particularly susceptible to cultural differences impacting how the competence is defined in the first place (e.g., refer back to the example of the differences between Western cultures and Mäori and Pacific peoples and the differing value placed on the notion of individually oriented behavior).

• Literacies and intelligent and applicable knowledge essentially denote the classical literacies, which are linked to language processing (e.g., the abilities to read, write, speak, listen, and understand) and basic numeracy. On a deeper level, they are linked to the use of mathematics, highly complex information processing, problem-solving, critical thinking, reflectivity, and metacognition. The main differences across countries arise in whether metacognition and using ICT (information and communication technology) are separate competence areas – perhaps, in the latter case, a new "basic literacy" – or whether they can be subsumed in this category.

- Learning competencies and lifelong learning imply technical, methodological, strategic, and motivational dimensions. For instance, it requires "conscious expertise in relation to one's own learning," the ability to transfer knowledge both horizontally and in depth, and, as the Flemish report described, "having the courage to explore and being eager to learn" (Dunon, 2001, p. 9).

- Communication competencies, which are sometimes subsumed under the "social competencies" heading, include both a cognitive, or more instrumental or technical, aspect (i.e., being able to maintain discourse, interact in discussions, defend a personal opinion) and an emotional one (i.e., being able to empathize or relate to others), which arguably enables "true" dialogue. The degree to which foreign language communication competencies are incorporated in this category, however, differs across countries.

Other areas of concern appearing less consistently across the lists are

- value orientation, a wide-ranging area that encompasses personal virtues such as integrity, responsibility, caring, and honesty; the acceptance of universal ethical norms; and, with less frequency, spirituality and religion;

- self-competence/self-management, which can refer both to action-oriented competencies such as self-regulation and to reflection-oriented competencies such as developing and expressing a sense of self;

- political or civic competencies, which imply the individual and collective competencies that reinforce democratic civic life from the neighborhood to the nation and which include dimensions such as exercising rights and responsibilities and valuing social justice or peaceful conflict resolution; and

- ecological awareness and behavior, an area which includes knowledge, attitudes, and actions regarding the environment and humans' interaction with it.

Competence areas related to culture, such as aesthetics, creativity, intercultural exchange or media, or to health, fitness, and sports, are mentioned infrequently. Trier (2003) finds this fairly surprising and concerning, considering the amount of time we devote to cultural activities and the importance of health awareness, attitudes, habits, and physical self-image.

Limits to formal synthesis

Although there are many commonalities and interrelationships among the lists of key competencies, and the aggregation presented above offers a valuable overview of areas of particular interest and relevance in a number of OECD countries, a synthesis of the various lists does not yield a coherent, logical system. The lists of competencies put forward in the CCP reports are mostly the result of a pragmatic approach; they reflect consensus-building in specific contexts and, as Helen Haste (2001) reminds us, are often driven both by the values that are held in high regard by the discussants responsible for identifying them and by the deficits that are perceived in need of remedy.

Thus, rather than following formal definitional constraints, many of the lists include items that belong to different conceptual levels or are situated at different degrees of generality or follow different criteria of categorization (Rychen, 2003). The same list may include demand-driven competencies (e.g., technological competence), cognitive skills (e.g., analytical skills), and values (e.g., honesty, ecological awareness), as well as competence areas related to particular social fields (e.g., cultural, political, health, or environmental competence). Moreover, Oates (2003) points out that most competence lists – which are typically developed through a consensual rather than a research process – fail to distinguish between commonly occurring skills, generic skills which contribute to effective performance in a wide range of settings, skills of transfer from one setting to another, and skills which are currently uncommon but likely to be needed in the future. If key competencies are to be sound bases for either assessment or curriculum development, Oates argues, there is a need to ground them with a firm theoretical foundation.

In closing, it is clear that, at a very basic level, the concept of key competence and the notion of "what people can do" is a highly relevant policy topic in many countries. The concept of key competence is used by policymakers and other individuals and groups to articulate and advance their particular agendas in various sectors and in various milieus. Furthermore, there is a great deal of convergence in the competencies that are identified as important or "key." The following chapters will discuss issues related to competencies and key competencies against this background and address how to identify key competencies both from an interdisciplinary perspective and based on theoretical work.

Chapter 2

A holistic model of competence
Dominique Simone Rychen and Laura Hersh Salganik

Introduction

Reviews of various initiatives (Oates, 2003, Trier, 2003; Weinert, 2001) reveal a lack of rigor and consistency in the use of terms related to competence. In public discourse and sometimes also in specialized literature, there is a tendency to use terms such as skill, qualification, competence, and literacy, either imprecisely or interchangeably, in order to describe what individuals must learn, know, or be able to do to succeed in school, at the workplace, or in social life. Minimal or no attention is devoted to defining the various notions or to distinguishing among them. For instance, in the economic field, the terms *skills* and *competencies* tend to be used synonymously, embracing "a broad definition of skills that includes not only cognitive skills but also noncognitive skills such as perseverance" (Levy & Murnane, 2001, p. 183).

DeSeCo's full title, *Definition and Selection of Competencies: Theoretical and Conceptual Foundations*, sets it apart from many other related activities, including those described in the previous chapter. In contrast to these efforts, in which semantic and conceptual subtleties have not been at the forefront, DeSeCo begins by taking a step back to define the concept of competence. OECD constituencies, recognizing the need for solid theoretical and conceptual foundations for defining, selecting, and assessing competencies that matter socially and economically, welcomed and supported DeSeCo's theory-oriented approach to competence.

Our premise is that notions and concepts do not contain their definitions in and of themselves; they are social constructs that can facilitate the understanding of reality while also constructing it in a manner that reflects and reinforces prevailing ideological assumptions and values. Thus, defining explicitly the meaning and nature of competence constitutes a crucial step in enabling a coherent and substantial discourse on competencies from a lifelong learning perspective.

A review of theory-grounded approaches to the concept of competence (Weinert, 2001) reveals that there is no single use of the concept of competence and no broadly accepted definition or unifying theory. Multiple and varied definitions of competence exist in social science literature. In line with Weinert's recommendation and subsequent discussions within the project, we opted for what he called a "conceptual pragmatism" in the sense of defining the term competence in a scientifically plausible and pragmatically relevant way.

The first section of this chapter presents a definition of the concept of competence that is relevant for policy, practice, and research (both theoretical and empirical). The second section elaborates on this concept and distinguishes it from other similarly used terms and ideas. The chapter ends with a discussion of the ramifications of this concept for policy.

The concept of competence

A functional approach to competence...

A competence is defined as the ability to successfully meet complex demands in a particular context through the mobilization of psychosocial prerequisites (including both cognitive and noncognitive aspects). This represents a demand-oriented or functional approach to defining competencies.[1] The primary focus is on the results the individual achieves through an action, choice, or way of behaving, with respect to the demands, for instance, related to a particular professional position, social role, or personal project.

Two examples taken from the scholarly contributions to DeSeCo illustrate the demand-oriented approach: Finding and sustaining community links is structured around the demands associated with forming communities in high-technology societies (Haste, 2001), and working in groups in the workplace allows workers to meet the demands associated with the changing organization of firms (Levy & Murnane, 2001). The National Vocational Qualifications (NVQs) in England and the national occupational profiles in Germany are examples of characterizations of demands referenced to particular occupations (Oates, 2003).

This functional approach to competence has the advantage of placing the complex demands and challenges that individuals encounter in the context of work and in everyday life at the forefront of the concept. As Weinert (2001) has pointed out, a demand-oriented approach does not depend on a comprehensive sociological classification of individual and social demands, but it does require a typical or specific characterization of classes of demands, performance criteria, and indicators of competencies. For this, curriculum theory, measurement models, task profiles for vocations, and task profiles for typical life situations (e.g., interaction with the mass media, leisure behavior, social conventions) provide valuable information.

---

[1] For a more comprehensive discussion of this issue, see Weinert (2001) and Witt and Lehmann (2001).

...with its internal structure

This functional, demand-oriented approach to competence has implications for the conceptualization of competence. As Ralf Witt and Rainer Lehmann (2001) have argued, "Without the functional approach no consideration of relevance is possible for competencies; without research on internal structures, no barriers can be provided against the temptations and traps of mere 'ability-to' expressions" (p. 5). Thus, the demand-oriented approach needs to be complemented by a conceptualization of competencies as internal mental structures in the sense of abilities, dispositions, or resources embedded in the individual. As illustrated in figure 1, these various dynamically interrelated components are defined by the characteristics of complex demands encountered in life (Weinert, 2001).

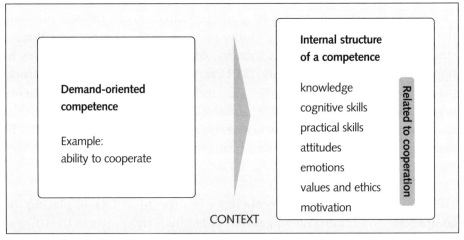

Figure 1: The demand defines the internal structure of a competence

Source: DeSeCo

For instance, in the IEA Civic Education Study, knowledge (of democratic principles), skills (in interpreting political communication), attitudes (related to trust in public institutions, the nation, opportunities for women, and political rights), and expectations for participation (in civic-related activities) are all regarded as relevant to meeting the demands of civic participation in democratic societies (Fratczak-Rudnicka & Torney-Purta, 2003; Torney-Purta, Lehmann, Oswald, & Schulz, 2001).

The components of the internal competence structure encompass a wide range of attributes. There is no question that cognitive skills or intellectual abilities (such as analytical or critical thinking skills, decision-making skills, or general problem-solving skills) and the knowledge base constitute crucial mental resources that need to be mobilized for competent performance or effective action. However, there is a broad agreement that meeting a demand or accomplishing a goal also requires the mobilization of social and behavioral components such as motivation, emotions, and values (see Canto-Sperber & Dupuy, 2001; Haste, 2001; Perrenoud, 2001; Witt & Lehmann, 2001). Oates (1999), emphasizing the importance of the full range of resources needed for competent performance, states that job profiles that gloss over the importance of both values and underpinning knowledge do not adequately capture the attributes needed for successful performance. This holistic apprehension of competence is supported by recent findings from neuroscience, namely, "that reasoning and emotion are vitally connected" (Gonczi, 2003, section 4). Possessing a competence means that one not only possesses the component resources, but is also able to *mobilize* such resources properly and to *orchestrate* them, at an appropriate time, in a complex situation (Le Boterf, 1994, 1997).

This approach is consistent with the action competence model described by Weinert (2001), which combines components that together represent a complex control system and result in a person taking action: "The theoretical construct of action competence comprehensively combines those intellectual abilities, content-specific knowledge, cognitive skills, domain-specific strategies, routines and subroutines, motivational tendencies, volitional control systems, personal value orientations, and social behaviors into a complex system" (p. 51).

...and context-dependency

The underlying assumption of our model of competence is that the relationship between the individual and society is dialectical and dynamic. Individuals do not operate in a social vacuum. Actions always take place in a social or socio-cultural environment, in a context that is structured into multiple social fields (such as the political field, the fields of work, of health, of family), each consisting of a structured set of social positions dynamically organized around a given set of social interests and challenges. It is within these fields that demands and the criteria for effective perform-ance and action take form and manifest themselves, and individuals act to meet them. The necessary contextualization of competence echoes well with situated learning theory, which views competence as inseparable from the context in which it is developed and used (Gonczi, 2003; Oates, 2003), and with cognitive science research, which rejects the distinction between what is stored in the brain and what exists in the environment. Andrew Gonczi (section 5) writes, "To clarify, it is not that the patterns [of mental resources] are stored in the mind, rather they are in the environment and that our brain interacts with the environment to produce the appropriate pattern, i.e., to act intelligently and competently." Thus, because compe-tence is a product of the interaction of attributes of individuals and the con-text in which they operate, "scrutiny of the 'characteristics' of the individ-ual alone is insufficient to explain effective performance in a range of settings" (Oates, section 4.1).

In summary, the underlying model of competence adopted by DeSeCo is holistic and dynamic in that it combines complex demands, psychosocial prerequisites (including cognitive, motivational, ethical, volitional, and social components), and context into a complex system that makes compe-tent performance or effective action possible. Thus, competencies do not exist independently of action and context. Instead, they are conceptualized in relation to demands and actualized by actions (which implies intentions, reasons, and goals) taken by individuals in a particular situation.

Elaboration and clarification

The complexity of the nature of competence as defined here raises a number of issues that call for further elaboration and clarification. A detailed discussion of these issues is, however, beyond the scope of this publication. Readers who are interested in further analysis are referred to other DeSeCo publications (in particular, Gonzci, 2003; Keating, 2003; Oates, 2003; and Weinert, 2001) and to the references they cite.

Transfer and adaptation

The notion that context is an integral element of competent performance raises the issue of whether an individual who is competent to meet a demand in one context or situation would be able to meet a similar demand in another context. Frequently, this topic is addressed in terms of *transfer*, the benefit obtained from having had previous experience in acquiring a new competence or performing successfully in a new situation. This raises the question of when a situation is new. As Oates (2003) points out, every situation we face is in one way or another different and new. Some of the differences may be trivial, some may be significant – and the significance of these differences can vary from person to person.

The disparity between existing competencies and competencies needed to meet new demands is resolved through *adaptation* (Oates, 2003). This approach leads away from the notion of transfer in the sense of transferring a skill or a competence from an old situation to a new one to a conception in which the adaptation of existing skills or competencies to meet the demands of new contexts is at the center. This understanding is consistent with Piaget's assertion that effective performance is a function of the dialectical interaction between existing competencies of the individual and demands of the new situation or context (Oates). In cases where competencies are applied in different domains of life, adaptation entails actively and reflectively using the knowledge, skills, or strategies developed in one social field, analyzing the new field, and translating and adapting the original knowledge, skills, or strategies to the demands of the new situation.

Observation of competence

A competence is manifested in actions, behaviors, or choices in particular situations or contexts. These actions, behaviors, or choices can be observed and measured, but the competence that underlies the performance, as well as the multiple attributes that contribute to it, can only be inferred (Gonzci, 2003; Oates, 2003; Weinert, 2001). Stated another way, attributions of competence (i.e., that an individual possesses a certain level of competence) are fundamentally inferences, made on the basis of evidence provided by observations of performance.

"What evidence is necessary to infer that a competence exists?" becomes a critical question. For example, it could be argued that, because of the contextual nature of competence, competence in one context cannot be inferred from evidence gathered in a different context. Oates (2003) and Gonczi (2003) suggest that evidence of competence is strengthened when relevant behaviors are observed multiple times and in a number of settings. In addition, Weinert (2001) argues that because performance depends on both cognitive and noncognitive prerequisites, it is important to account for the range of critical dimensions that make up a competence (including cognitive skills and motivational, ethical, and emotional aspects) when making inferences about competencies.

Levels of competence

Defining competencies with regard to the demands that individuals and societies face raises the question of what levels of competence are adequate or necessary in order to cope with these manifold and multifaceted demands. Robert Kegan (2001) proposes a progression of competence levels based on a theoretical perspective from developmental psychology that describes how individuals' "ways of knowing" change through childhood and into adulthood. Increasing levels of competence are associated with the gradual development of mental complexity. Roughly during adolescence, for instance, individuals develop the ability to think abstractly, construct values and ideals through self-reflection, and subordinate their own interests to those of another person or group. A higher level of mental complexity is reached when adults can step back from the "socialization press" and make their own judgments (see chapter 3).

Because the notion of competence refers to a particular level of ability – i.e., individuals are described as competent when they achieve a certain level of expertise or ability – competencies and competence-related components are assumed to exist on continua (see chapter 5). Underlying this notion is a theoretical scale, ranging from low to high, that describes the difficulty level of demands an individual is facing. Whenever judgments are made about competence (e.g., in the case of assessments), it is therefore not a matter of finding out whether an individual does or does not possess a particular competence or component, but rather of determining where along the continuum from low to high an individual's performance falls. For future assessments, it will be important to include the complete range of competence levels, including the one that reflects the higher order of mental complexity necessary to cope with the demands of modern life.

Competencies are learned

It is important to make explicit that competencies are assumed to be learnable and teachable. "Learning processes are a necessary condition for the acquisition of prerequisites for successful mastery of complex demands" (Weinert, 2001, p. 63). Weinert recognizes that at times notions related to ability and competence are used to describe characteristics that "are part of the basic cognitive apparatus and as such are not learned prerequisites for reaching specific performance goals" (pp. 59–60). He recommends that the system of primary cognitive abilities, which are innate and not learned, be distinguished from learned, demand-specific competencies and that the notion of competence should refer to those abilities that can be learned and taught.

Individual and collective competence

Within the DeSeCo Project, the focus has been on the *individual* rather than on the *collective* concept of competence. The latter focuses on demands facing groups of individuals or institutions, such as teams, firms, organizations, communities, or nations. For an organization to be competent, that is, to meet the demands facing it, its members may need a range of competencies, but each individual may not need them all (Weinert, 2001). The conception of collective competence raises fundamental questions not answered in DeSeCo related to the division of labor, the distribution of resources, and principles of equal opportunity and justice (see chapter 4). Other issues concern interrelationships between structural and institutional factors and collective competence, and the manner in which collective competence is the result of a dialectical relationship between the competencies of individuals and the structural and institutional characteristics of the context. Depending on the cultural context, collective competence may also serve as a reference point for individuals' judgments about their own competence, with individuals attributing to themselves what they view as the competence of the group (Featherman & Carson, 1999).

DeSeCo's decision to focus on individually based competencies does not mean that demands facing groups or communities are excluded from consideration. Many of the complex demands of modern life indeed imply interactions among individuals and groups. This is reflected in one of the three categories of key competence (discussed in chapter 3), interacting in socially heterogeneous groups. The competencies put forth in this category (the ability to relate well to others, to cooperate or work in teams, and to manage and solve conflicts) are conceived of as individual competencies everyone should acquire and develop.

Competencies, skills, and personal qualities

Reviews of literature in both the research and policy arenas reveal that there is often little definitional and conceptual distinction between the terms *competencies* and *skills* and that attributes often characterized as personal qualities also appear on lists of competencies (Weinert, 2001; see also chapter 1). Clarifying the meaning and usage of these terms in relation to the concept of competence delineated above can benefit and facilitate further discussion of competence and related topics.

First, the terms *competence* and *skill* are not synonyms. Although occasionally the term *skill* is used in a manner that is quite similar, even identical, to the notion of competence,[2] more often it carries meanings and connotations that are quite different: for instance, skills as being decomposed into abstract rules and algorithms (Canto-Sperber & Dupuy, 2001), skills as fully automatized (Weinert, 2001), or skills as "an ability to perform complex motor and/or cognitive acts with ease, precision, and adaptability to changing conditions" (Weinert, 1999, p. 35). The term skills also at times refers to a relatively low difficulty level, as is often the case with the term *basic skills*.[3] Each of these conceptions is clearly inconsistent with the concept and notion of competence as a complex action system encompassing cognitive skills, attitudes, and other noncognitive components and irreducible to its component parts.

Second, the term *competence* is also sometimes used to refer to general personal qualities such as honesty, integrity, and responsibility. These qualities, however, are usually not associated with a specific type of demand. The same is true for values and ethics or motivational aspects, which constitute general foundations of particular competencies, but are not competencies themselves.

---

[2] For instance, in reference to activities associated with noncognitive domains, such as teamwork skills or social skills.

[3] Basic skills, however, do not always refer to low-level skills. In the U.S. Secretary's Commission on Achieving Necessary Skills (SCANS) project, reading, writing, arithmetic and mathematics, and speaking and listening are identified as basic skills, but here *basic* indicates that they are a base for other skills rather than indicating a level of difficulty. For example, reading includes being able to "judge the accuracy, appropriateness, style, and plausibility of reports, proposals, or theories of other writers"; mathematics includes being able to "understand the role of chance in the occurrence and prediction of events"; speaking includes being able to "understand and respond to listener feedback; and ask questions when needed" (U.S. Department of Labor, 1992, p. 83).

To illustrate, with regard to demands such as "cooperate with others" or "use technology or information effectively," we would evoke the term competence rather than skill, assuming – from a holistic perspective – that a range of mental prerequisites needs to be mobilized. On the other hand, if the focus – be it in assessment or teaching practice – is only on a single component (for instance, cognitive functioning or motivation), then the term competence would indeed be inappropriate. Neither cognitive components nor motivational aspects alone make up a competence. For example, critical thinking skills, analytical skills, general problem-solving skills, and persistence would not be considered competencies because they do not describe an individual's complete response to a demand. They constitute, however, valuable, if not indispensable, components of action competence.

Competence and literacy

Like competence, the notion of *literacy* is currently enjoying widespread use in education policy discourse. Traditionally, the word literacy referred to the level of reading and writing skills needed for a minimal functioning in society; an individual was considered either to be literate (above the cutoff) or illiterate (below the cutoff), with no possibility of expressing gradations beyond the dichotomy. In the 1990s, the International Adult Literacy Survey (IALS) introduced to the policy discourse in OECD countries a new conception of literacy that represented a significant shift from previous usages of the term, building the assessment around the notions that literacy allows individuals to achieve their goals and develop their knowledge and potential, and that it exists on a continuum (OECD & Human Resources Development Canada, 1995; Salganik, 2001).

More recently, the Programme for International Student Assessment (PISA) adopted literacy as a unifying concept across the subject-area domains (e.g., PISA assesses reading, mathematical, and scientific literacy). The literacy concept directs the assessment away from an exclusive focus on curricular content and toward reflecting on knowledge, achieving personal goals, and participating effectively in society (OECD, 2000).

The use of this expanded concept of literacy in international assessments and also in the policy arena[4] has not, however, eliminated many of the terminological difficulties stemming from numerous and imprecise uses of the word, difficulties similar to those encountered with the use of competence (see Weinert, 2001, pp. 45–46). Furthermore, translating *literacy* into other languages has proven problematic, and even in English it is generally associated with the cognitive realm and rarely directly conveys the intended conceptual centrality of meeting complex demands through mobilizing a range of mental prerequisites.

The convergence between the concept of literacy as defined in current assessment frameworks and DeSeCo's concept of competence, and the difficulties associated with the term literacy, together suggest that international assessments would benefit from replacing the concept of literacy with the concept of competence. An added advantage would be that such a change would be consistent with the political discourse at the level of the OECD education ministers, as reflected in their communiqué "Investing in Competencies for All" (OECD, 2001b), which states that "sustainable development and social cohesion depend critically on the competencies of all of our population – with competencies understood to cover knowledge, skills, attitudes, and values" (p. 2).

Competence and key competence

Terms such as key competencies, core competencies, key qualifications, and life or core skills enjoy much popularity in the social sciences and in education policy. Generally, the terms refer to "multifunctional and transdisciplinary competencies that are useful for achieving many important goals, mastering different tasks, and acting in unfamiliar situations" (Weinert, 2001, p. 52). In the Adult Literacy and Life Skills Survey (ALL), life skills are defined as "skills or abilities individuals need in order to achieve success in life, within the context of their socio-cultural milieu, through adaptation to, shaping of, and selection of environments" (Binkley, Sternberg, Jones, & Nohara, 1999, p. 3).

---

[4] A few examples are health literacy, media literacy, family literacy, and environmental literacy.

In line with DeSeCo's objective to focus on competencies that are of particular importance, the notion of key competencies is used – to start with – as
a synonym for critical or important competencies. As will be discussed in
more detail in the next chapter, DeSeCo conceives of key competencies as
individually based competencies that contribute to a successful life and a
well-functioning society, are relevant across different spheres of life, and are
important for all individuals. Consistent with the broad concept of competence, each key competence is a combination of interrelated cognitive skills,
attitudes, motivation and emotion, and other social components.

Competencies that do not meet all of the criteria above are not considered
key competencies. Thus, competencies that are relevant or important for
only some individuals – for example, teaching modern history or cultivat-
ing mussels and oysters – are not deemed key competencies. These competencies may be important for a successful life for some, but they are clearly
not important for everyone. In addition, they are work- or job-specific and
thus do not meet the condition of applying across multiple social fields.

Oates (2003) cautions against the interpretation that key competencies provide the complete range of resources needed to meet demands in a particular context or occupation. Clearly, whatever is defined and identified as a
key competence, it will not be sufficient, as pointed out by Weinert (2001),

> *to possess some key competencies, to have learned how to
> learn, and to acquire some media competence so that
> necessary information can be acquired at any time in an
> electronic form... Modern cognitive psychology would tell
> us that such an educational model is not only a utopia,
> but also mostly nonsense.* (p. 53)

Thus, DeSeCo's focus on key competencies does not question the importance of other competencies. Key competencies do not substitute for
domain-specific competencies, which are also necessary and often constitute important resources for coping with the demands of particular contexts
and situations.

Assessment of competence

The complex nature of competencies and their inseparability from context have important implications for the assessment of competence. First, competence cannot be directly measured or observed, but must be inferred from observing performance to meet a demand in a number of settings (Oates, 2003). It must be recognized that large-scale assessments, even those that are "performance-based," are only approximations of the demands individuals face in real life. A number of strategies have been suggested to narrow the gap between assessment tasks and real-life demands on individuals. These include using a wide range of material from situations in real life,[5] validating assessment results by showing that they predict successful outcomes apart from the assessment (Weinert, 2001), and designing assessments to include different contexts or settings that require individuals to adapt to similar demands in the context of the assessment (Oates).

In addition, most assessments of competencies – including classroom testing in schools and large-scale assessments – have traditionally been restricted to the cognitive components of competence. Weinert (2001) cautions against restricting attention on assessments to cognitive elements of competencies if one is concerned with individuals' ability to meet demands across a range of fields, noting that comparative measurements require scales to measure both cognitive and noncognitive elements (see chapter 5).

The fact that competence must be inferred from performance is at the root of a fundamental critique of assessment, which argues that specifying assessment tasks is not a neutral exercise:

---

[5] PISA and ALL, for example, use this approach.

> *There is clearly a power dimension that animates these concerns. If I set the task demands (a functionalist operation), then I am empowered to make inferences about your competence based on your performance, whereas you are compelled to try to maximize your performance in order to persuade me of your competence. This is the precise power differential that is revealed as one moves from population indicators to accountability or selection regimes. It is generally non-problematic for elites or for those who hold power, but if the goal is to move toward broader enhancement of competencies, this power differential cannot be ignored.* (Keating, 2003, section 3.2)

These considerations pose a major challenge and important responsibility for those who are engaged in designing and interpreting assessments of competencies.

Implications for policy: Toward competencies for all

The concept of competence developed in DeSeCo has important implications for policy and raises questions about the adequacy and effectiveness of traditional teaching and learning methods. Although not a main focus of DeSeCo, many issues related to competence development and, specifically, education policy have been addressed in the written contributions to DeSeCo and were raised at the 2nd international symposium. Here, we can only sketch some of the practical implications and issues at stake as potential topics for further consideration.

Strategies to promote learning

How can competencies be developed and enhanced? What are the implications for schools – modern societies' primary institution responsible for teaching and learning – as they seek to foster and enhance competence and key competencies for all? Schools have traditionally emphasized transmission of knowledge and cognitive skills through discipline-based curricula. In this long-standing model, teachers, who have the knowledge, are entrusted with imparting that knowledge to students, who do not have it. In most cases, students have relatively little input about how schools are run or what their everyday life in school is like.

Gonczi (2003) strongly questions this traditional notion of learning in terms of filling up the mind of the learner with facts, knowledge, beliefs, and ideas as if the mind were a container.

> *The old learning paradigm needs to be replaced by a new*
> *one which links learners to the environment in which*
> *learning is taking place. Such a conception of learning*
> *takes account of the affective, moral, physical, as well as*
> *cognitive aspects of individuals and insists that real*
> *learning only takes place in and through action. Hence*
> *the learning of key competences can only occur through*
> *acting on the world in ways that increase the capacity to*
> *make judgments – presumably over the life span.* (section 1)

He points to projects piloted in Australia in the 1990s as examples of school-based activities consistent with this model of learning (Gonczi, 2003). They include encouraging active independent learning in ways that simulate later life contexts. Underlying this approach is situated learning theory, which argues that knowledge is developed or created in learners through actions taken in a range of contexts (Lave & Wenger, 1990). Gonczi also recommends integrating the teaching of key competencies with the teaching of other material and making key competencies explicit even when integrated into other activities.

Further, the concept of competence highlights the importance of ensuring that what is taught makes sense to individuals and enables them to meet demands encountered in different contexts. For this, the notion of adaptability is critical. Studies have shown that some learning strategies not only increase adaptability, which is associated with deep learning rather than short-term recall, but also motivation and autonomy. Effective learning strategies include using a wide range of contexts, inductive rather than deductive processes, problem-based learning contexts in which problems are integrated rather than broken into discrete, artificial elements, and encouragement of self-directed learning and self-reflection on learning styles (Oates, 2003, section 3.2).

DeSeCo's finding that meeting complex demands in and across social fields (see chapter 3) implies an overall development of critical thinking and a reflective approach based on formal and informal knowledge and experience in life calls for more than altering or expanding school curricula or programs. Rather, it requires

> *a fairly significant shift in the teacher-student relationship and the functioning of educational establishments towards the 'self-government' type of education. What has to be envisioned, therefore, is a high-risk education, necessitating changes in attitudes and learning/teaching commitments…as much as changes in the curriculum.*
> (Perrenoud, 2001, p. 147)

In the area of developing civic competencies, the IEA Civic Education Study found that in the majority of countries, the extent to which students reported that an open, trusting climate existed in their classrooms was a predictor of whether the students expected to vote in political elections in the future and also of several other measures, such as civic knowledge and students' confidence in their ability to be effective participants in decisions influencing their school (Fratczak-Rudnicka & Torney-Purta, 2003).

Thus, for individuals to reach the higher level of mental complexity necessary to meet the demands of modern life, schools must provide their students the support to master a challenging curriculum over time. "No school presents its students with a curriculum they can master immediately" (Kegan, 2001, p. 203). Further, since individuals typically do not reach this competence level until adulthood, educational experiences and opportunities for learning and mental development need to be provided into the adult years to allow "not only the acquisition of skills or an increase in one's fund of knowledge, but education for development, education for transformation" (p. 203). For Kegan, this understanding provides an important foundation for the purpose of adult or lifelong education.

A favorable environment

The acquisition of competencies cannot be the responsibility only of the individual and cannot be reduced to a matter of personal effort, motivation, and learning skills. The development and actualization of competencies are contingent upon the existence of a favorable material, institutional, and social environment. Economic and social policies, in particular, education policy, are challenged to provide adequate opportunities for both young people and adults not only to learn the necessary competencies but also to use them. In fact, "if societies do not afford their citizens meaningful opportunities to use the competencies that they have and value, then erosion rather than enhancement of competencies is the more likely outcome" (Keating, 2003, section 2.3.5).

To date, social policy with respect to human capital has focused on schooling and economic outcomes. However, building a genuine learning society that strives for sustainable development requires more. It necessitates "a shift to equal consideration of societal affordances...for renewing, retaining, and reinforcing competencies throughout the population" (Keating, 2003, section 2.3.5).

A complete analysis would need to include, at least, consideration of family policies; policies affecting workplace participation, learning, and renewal of competencies; policies affecting the quality of the social and physical environment where people live and work; health and health care policies; and policies dealing with retirement, activities of older citizens and elder care. (Keating, 2003, section 2.2.4)

Further, a learning society would involve all social institutions that have a learning dimension and a responsibility for the growth and development of their members, such as schools, workplaces, families, trade unions, clubs, and professional associations (Gonczi, 2003, section 12). The appropriate "division of work," however, among the various institutions is not obvious. The specific roles each one can play in enhancing the development of key competencies – and partnerships among them – need to be clarified based on sound conceptual and theoretical foundations. This would suggest that efforts directed at individually based competencies would need to be complemented by an analysis of the actual and desirable competencies of institutions: How can social institutions provide an enabling environment for the actualization of individually based key competencies and contribute to a well-functioning, sustainable society?

This chapter has focused on formalizing a definition of competence highlighting the centrality of demands, psychosocial prerequisites of individuals, and context. This holistic model of competence is theoretically grounded and constitutes a critical element of DeSeCo's overarching frame of reference by laying out a conceptual foundation for defining and selecting key competencies.

Chapter 3

Key competencies: Meeting important challenges in life

Dominique Simone Rychen

Introduction

From the start, DeSeCo was faced with a number of questions and critiques regarding the construction of a limited set of key competencies of international relevance. Philippe Perrenoud, a sociologist, provocatively entitled his contribution to the first international DeSeCo symposium in 1999, "Identifying universal core competencies: Technocratic fantasy or an extension of human rights?" And Jack Goody (2001), an anthropologist, challenged the project by denying that a limited set of competencies valid in and across nations and social fields could be found. His argument was based on the observation that cultures, ways of life and skills, or the way these skills are defined and valued, vary enormously from one society to another, among groups, and over time. This argument is reinforced by the fact that, even within the OECD member countries, one encounters a great deal of diversity in cultures, value systems, political and economic priorities, living conditions, and ways of life, both across and within national borders. These differences suggest significant variation in demands placed on societies, institutions, organizations, and individuals.

With the myriad of conceivable individual and social differences in and across countries, is there any ground for defining a general (or universally applicable) set of key competencies? To what extent is the basic premise, that a limited number of common key competencies can be constructed, even justified? Various contributions to DeSeCo yield an important response: Diversity does not preclude claims of common visions, shared ideals, and a recognition of global processes and challenges.

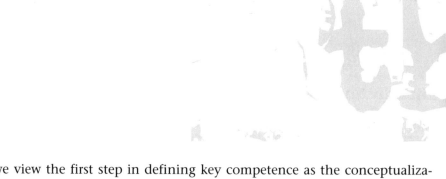

If we view the first step in defining key competence as the conceptualization of competence (see chapter 2), the second step must be to describe what makes a competence "key." The notion of key competence is not new, but in recent years it has become especially popular among social scientists and education policy-makers in many OECD countries (see chapter 1). This increased interest has brought with it a variety of definitions and proposed lists of key competencies, but little conceptual consistency and theoretical grounding (Oates, 2003). Although some commonalities do exist, the many differences make it difficult to infer or synthesize a formalized definition of key competence or a formalized distinction between the terms *competence* and *key competence*. Furthermore, as has been observed in the DeSeCo country reports (Trier, 2003), the term *key competencies* is often used interchangeably with the terms *core competencies, skills,* or *educational goals.* Weinert (2001) describes the situation in the following terms:

> *The concept of key competence is…no less vague and ambiguous than the concept of competence. Clear and well-reasoned distinctions between the two concepts are either arbitrary or nonexistent. Within the last few years over 650 different key competencies have been suggested just in the German literature on occupational training. These competencies range from such constructs as creativity, logical thinking, problem-solving skills, achievement readiness, independence, and concentration abilities, to foreign language skills, communications skills, and media competencies.* (pp. 51–52)

Clearly, if the term *key* is to have any meaning, credibility, or utility, there cannot be 650 key competencies. Thus, a major goal of the DeSeCo Project has been to stimulate and review expert opinions in order to put forth some explicit criteria and requirements for key competencies. Such a definition must be relevant and useful in research as well as in policy and practice, and should provide a basis for selecting key competencies in an international context.

This chapter presents critical elements of DeSeCo's overarching frame of reference for key competencies: the definition of key competencies, the competence level required in light of the complex demands individuals and societies are facing today, and a three-fold categorization of key competencies as a conceptual basis for mapping and describing key competencies. A number of individually based key competencies are highlighted within the three-fold categorization. Finally, recognizing that contextual variation is a key issue, a model for thinking about how key competencies function in different situations is addressed in the last section of the chapter.

Definition of key competencies

Using the definitional criteria for the competence model described in chapter 2, one could imagine any number of competencies. Not all, however, would generate widespread interest and support for their monitoring and development, especially from a policy perspective. Policy-makers would presumably not wish to devote valuable resources to the development of competencies that have little impact on the well-being of individuals or society or to competencies that are already considered to be widely held. There are, therefore, compelling reasons to distinguish between competence and key competence, with *key* used, to begin with, as a synonym for *critical* or *important*. Naturally, then, the follow-up question is "important for what?"

Based upon a review of existing work in the area of competence and on the input of experts from a variety of backgrounds, the concept of key competence as defined in DeSeCo relies on three general criteria, namely, that *key competencies*

...contribute to highly valued outcomes at the individual and societal levels in terms of an overall successful life and a well-functioning society.
This conception is consistent with the importance placed on human and social capital for personal, economic, and social well-being. Recent research reinforces the view that not only does human capital play a critical role in

economic performance (e.g., Levy & Murnane, 2001), but also that important individual and social benefits flow from investment in human capital, such as better health, improved well-being, better parenting, and increased social and political engagement (OECD, 2001d).

...are instrumental for meeting important, complex demands and challenges in a wide spectrum of contexts.
Individuals participate in many different spheres of activity. There is no doubt that in order to function well or perform successfully – as an employer or employee, a consumer, a citizen, a student, a family member – different domain- or role-specific competencies are required or are desirable. The focus of DeSeCo, however, has been on competencies that are thought to be instrumental for coping with important individual and social demands in a wide spectrum of contexts. Thus, key competencies aim to enable individuals to navigate and participate effectively in and across multiple social fields, such as the economic sector, political life, social relations and the family, public and private interpersonal relations, and the health field. This means that key competencies are not specific to only one domain; they are transversal in the sense that they apply to multiple areas of life.

...are important for all individuals.
This criterion reflects a political choice in the sense of a commitment to enhancing competencies that contribute to social equality rather than simply fostering the interests of an elite (Ridgeway, 2001). "This commitment is illustrated by the focus on learned skills rather than innate abilities and on competencies necessary for an adequate, meaningful life that could be available to all rather than one that will be inherently confined to an elite" (p. 205). Or, in the words of Perrenoud (2001): "What is the point of defining *basic* competencies unless it is to mobilize all the resources required to enable all citizens to acquire them, first and foremost those who are at present failing to acquire them?" (p. 121). Investing in competencies for all is also consistent with the general commitment of OECD countries (OECD, 2001b) to expand opportunities for all individuals in various spheres of life, to improve overall living conditions in society, and to invest in the development of competencies for all as a means to these ends.

The references to *a successful life, a well-functioning society*, and *complex demands* in this definition of key competence require further explanation regarding a general vision of, or an agreement on, societal goals and some key features that characterize the world in which competencies are applied. This is the topic of the following section.

A common vision of the world as a backdrop

"Economics values the development of hypotheses that can be empirically tested, and outcomes that can be measured with available data. As a result, most economic analysis focuses on the economy that exists – not an idealized economy that might exist" (Levy & Murnane, 2001, p. 151). However, "...if one wants to go beyond an individual's adaptation level to the world of today with its limited possibilities of further development, and change the world by providing people with the appropriate competencies, it is necessary to choose a normative starting point, and not an empirical one, when defining key competencies..." (Weinert, 2001, p. 53). Defining and selecting key competencies is not just an academic issue; normative considerations regarding the world and the individual play a role in what are considered important, desired, and valued outcomes.

Thus, tackling the seemingly straightforward research question "What competencies are relevant for an individual to lead a successful and responsible life and for society to face the challenges of the present and future?" raises, from the outset, even more profound questions, such as "What type of society do we imagine and desire?", "What constitutes a successful life?", and "Which social and economic developments are we referring to?" More importantly, the premise of DeSeCo requires us to look for answers that are relevant for all individuals in OECD member countries and, potentially, in transition and developing countries as well. Thus, a first step is an outline of some common goals and recognizable features of society and the world. Our description of commonalities, even if sketchy, provides a heuristic set of values, demands, and conditions that serve as a backdrop for defining and selecting key competencies.

A normative starting point

As noted by Delors and Draxler (2001), "the United Nations system and democratic governments...function on the assumption that there are certain ideas, values, and notions that we can agree upon and use to found collective enterprises" (p. 214). Thus, it is possible to begin our search for a common normative vision of the world with a number of adopted international conventions detailing objectives for global social reform and socio-economic development. Conventions and agreements – in particular, the Universal Declaration of Human Rights, the World Declaration on Education for All, and the Rio Declaration on Environment and Development – specify basic human rights, democratic values, and sustainable and integrated environmental, economic, and social development as desirable goals for all societies. For example, in defining the aim of educational development, the World Declaration on Education for All (1990), more than 10 years old, states in Article I that educational opportunities should help individuals "to survive, to develop their full capacities, to live and work in dignity, to participate fully in development, to improve the quality of their lives, to make informed decisions, and to continue learning." It further states that fulfilling educational needs

> *empowers individuals in any society and confers upon them a responsibility to respect and build upon their collective cultural, linguistic and spiritual heritage, to promote the education of others, to further the cause of social justice, to achieve environmental protection, to be tolerant towards social, political and religious systems which differ from their own, ensuring that commonly accepted humanistic values and human rights are upheld, and to work for international peace and solidarity in an interdependent world.* (Article I)

The assumption that there are common features and shared values that unite us is reinforced by the theoretical contribution to DeSeCo from the philosophical perspective of Monique Canto-Sperber and Jean-Pierre Dupuy (2001). Focusing on the ideal of the "good life," they state that not only do individuals have "many of the same physiological needs and capacities," but that "there are also psychological similarities," for instance:

> *They do not differ in their psychological aspirations to go beyond necessity, to do what is necessary for survival, and to aim at a condition in which they have leisure, choices, alternatives. We are alike in the capacity to learn from the past and plan for the future. We have a view, though never clearly articulated, about what we want to make out of our lives. We have the capacity to think, remember, imagine, have feelings and emotions, and to restrain ourselves. Contact with other people is part of human life; most of the time we depend on it.*
> (pp. 73–74)

The authors go on to identify key values that account for the good life in general and that are consistent with any major moral theory (Canto-Sperber & Dupuy, 2001, p. 75). The values of the good life, the philosophers say, include

- accomplishment;
- the elements of human existence ("choosing one's own course through life and having a life which is properly human");
- an understanding of oneself and one's world;
- enjoyment; and
- deep personal relations.

These values are general principles compatible with individual and social diversity. Many different forms of the good life are conceivable, depending on individual lifestyle and socio-economic and cultural context. Yet, it should be noted that the realization of these values still remains out of reach, particularly in developing countries, for large populations whose lives are reduced to a daily struggle for survival.

For our purpose (i.e., defining and selecting key competencies for a successful life and a well-functioning society), the assumed common values and the widespread acceptance of the international conventions means that universal objectives such as respect for human rights and sustainable development do exist and can serve as a regulative ideal and normative anchoring point for the discourse on key competencies. The more specific question "What are the particular dimensions of a successful life and a well-functioning society that key competencies contribute to and against which they will need to be validated?" will be addressed in chapter 4.

Common and global challenges

Within a common normative framework, countries and societies – even within the OECD – differ significantly in terms of economic and political goals and priorities, cultural traditions, environmental settings, available resources, and employment and social opportunities, thereby challenging the construction of a common set of key competencies (e.g., Goody, 2001). In spite of common values and principles at the general level, representations and beliefs can come into conflict when it comes to applying them in practice. Hence, the meaning and the concretization of individual and societal goals as well as the underlying hierarchies of values – and trade-offs between, at times, conflicting objectives – are influenced by socio-economic and cultural factors and contingent upon power relations and personal, social, or political choices and priorities (e.g., Carson, 2001).

Exclusively emphasizing diversity, differences, and variation risks drifting into relativism, which does not do justice to the social reality. Cultural diversity and socioeconomic inequalities traverse most, if not all, countries and often have similar origins. And whatever the differences between countries in occupations, workplaces, and social and political institutions, the fact is that these same settings and institutions exist in most – in many cases, all – countries and are often as similar as they are different. Thus, increasing individual and social diversity is only one common facet of our world. Increasing complexity and interdependence are other central features of today's world. As a result, societies and individuals are confronted with a plethora of old and new global problems and issues with varying effects and manifestations at all levels of life: substantial inequality of opportunities; poverty in its various forms; population movements;

economic changes; competition; ecological and political destabilization; disorganization of communities; new forms of communication, alienation, and violence; and so on. Some are related to particular forms of asymmetries in political, social, and economic power; others are more the result of recent globalization processes. For instance, economic and cultural globalization and the convergence of technology and production have given rise to fora of exchange and standards that are truly global. As evidence, one need only consider the rise of large-scale international movements, organizations, and corporations or the ease with which information and knowledge can be exchanged globally. Although the degree to which individuals have access to and participate in the "global village" varies widely (for many individuals and groups, the "global village" remains a myth),[1] its emergence exerts a powerful influence – for both better and worse – on national policies and initiatives.

The fact that we can point to numerous similarities within and across countries does not mean that they will automatically translate into meaningful key competencies, nor does it allow us to extrapolate key competencies for all OECD countries from those found in a single country (see chapter 1). Yet, as Frank Levy and Richard Murnane (2001) note, "the globalization of trade and the international spread of technology are strong forces pushing toward a global set of key competencies" (p. 170).

---

[1] Addressing important questions related to access to new technologies and standard products, and the distribution and benefits of such goods in relation to competence development, is beyond the scope of DeSeCo.

Referring to common values and goals as well as to wide-ranging global issues and problems does not deny diversity, but only asserts that there is enough similarity in the lives people lead to make the construction of a general set of key competencies useful.

Theoretical and conceptual foundations

In light of the definitional constraints for key competencies and against the backdrop of the broad societal goals and global challenges, we have focused our efforts on identifying concepts and theoretical models that can underpin the conceptualization of a general set of key competencies from an interdisciplinary perspective.

The first international DeSeCo symposium[2] – held in Neuchâtel, Switzerland, in October 1999 – and subsequent workshops provided important opportunities for intense debate and reflection among scholars and experts from multiple disciplines on common features that transcend the

[2] For information on the first international DeSeCo symposium, go to
  http://www.statistik.admin.ch/stat_ch/ber15/deseco/deseco_symp99.htm

particularities of the various approaches and inputs. What has emerged is a broad agreement on some general overarching concepts that give shape to a theory-grounded frame of reference for key competencies.

There are two key elements of this framework, in addition to the model of competence (see chapter 2) and the defining parameters noted above: first, the specification of the level of mental complexity required by modern life, based on an evolutionary model of the complexification of the mind (Kegan, 2001, p. 194); and, second, a three-fold categorization for key competencies that contribute to a successful life and a well-functioning society. We comprehend the required mental complexity via a concept of reflectivity (in the sense of a reflective approach to life on the part of the individual) and express our conception of key competencies in terms of three broad categories – interacting in socially heterogeneous groups, acting autonomously, and using tools interactively – all of which assume the development of the higher level of mental complexity.

The concept of reflectivity as a response to complex mental demands and the three-fold categorization for key competencies are the result of exchange, discussion, and analytical and creative work and, thus, represent an important transition in the DeSeCo Project from multidisciplinary perspectives to interdisciplinary comprehension and theorization.

This section begins with a description of the umbrella concept of reflectivity. Following that discussion, the three categories of key competencies are outlined as the model for translating the theoretical foundations (i.e., reflectivity and the underlying concepts of the categories) into the more tangible terms of action-oriented key competencies.

Reflective practice in the face of the complex demands of modern life

As noted above, our analysis and conceptualization of key competencies are grounded in a vision of the world as complex,[3] interdependent, and

---

[3] But as pointed out by Canto-Sperber and Dupuy (2001), "it must be acknowledged that a good deal of the contemporary human world, especially in its technological dimensions, is more complicated than complex" (pp. 79–82).

conflict-prone, affecting and challenging not only countries, communities, institutions, and organizations but, ultimately, the individual and his or her mind. Uncertainty is one of the consequences of a complex world, with implications for individuals. As, for instance, Carlo Callieri (2001) states:

> *Indeed, the problem is a world in which uncertainty is growing as situations become increasingly complex... Societies must equip themselves with tools that enable them to tackle complexity in a manageable way that conquers uncertainty. In this new perspective, the individual takes on an absolutely crucial function, creating the tools with which to manage uncertainty and turn it to his or her own advantage.* (p. 231)

The idea that individuals need not only respond to complex situations, but "create the tools" to do so, takes the idea of a competence well beyond that of a skill that can be applied repeatedly in the manner in which it was originally learned. Such skills may very well be needed, but current challenges require a level of competence that enables individuals to cope with innovation and continuity (see Haste, 2001; also Oates, 2003) and to go beyond simply "applying" competencies as if they were formulae or straightforward processes.

The issue of complexity, or related terms, is – like a leading theme – mirrored in various discourses on competencies and education goals. A review of the skills and competence lists available to DeSeCo suggests that much of what is identified as key competencies or educational goals goes well beyond recalling accumulated knowledge, thinking abstractly, and being well socialized (Trier, 2003; chapter 1). For coping with many of the demands of modern life, these are apparently not sufficient. As illustrated by Kegan (2001) and presented in several academic essays (Rychen & Salganik, 2001), coping with complex challenges as they manifest in and across multiple social fields calls for the development of a higher level of mental complexity or, in Kegan's terms (2001), the "self-authoring order of mental complexity." This mental order implies a critical stance and a reflective and holistic approach to life, enabling individuals "to learn from experience and think for themselves, without being prisoners of the exclusive thinking or expectations of their environment" (Perrenoud, 2001, p. 146).

Underlying reflectivity is the idea of an objectivation process: what was subject becomes object. "*Object* refers to those elements of our knowing or organizing that we can reflect on, handle, look at, be responsible for, relate to each other, take control of, internalize, assimilate, or otherwise operate upon... *Subject* refers to those elements of our knowing...that we are identified with, tied to, fused with, or embedded in" (Kegan, 1994, p. 32). In other words, and with important consequences for the development of key competencies, individuals can only be responsible for, in control of, or reflect upon that which is object.

According to Kegan (2001) – and reflected also in various scholarly essays – this "self-authoring order of mental complexity" requires that we

- gain some distance from the socializing press so that we can look at and make judgments about the expectations and claims that bombard us from all directions;

- take responsibility for the fact that we are the creators...of...feelings and thoughts – i.e., it is not enough to reflectively identify the origins of our dysfunctional behaviors, thoughts, and feelings in our early family experience, as if we could only become more astute audience members viewing the drama of our inner psychologies; rather we are expected as mature adults to become more like playwrights who can jump on stage and re-author the scripts of the dramas themselves; and

- create a more complex system of abstractions or values – a whole framework, theory, or ideology – which generates distinct abstractions or values, prioritizes them, and internally resolves conflicts among them. (p. 197)

In this perspective, requirements such as flexibility and adaptability, tolerance and open-mindedness, and responsibility and initiative, which are usually associated with a competent adult, take on particular meaning and underpin the necessity of conceiving key competences as involving a higher level of mental complexity.

To elucidate the meaning of reflectivity as the competence level required for coping with the mental challenges that confront adults in many life situations, three conceptual illustrations are presented below – navigating in social space, dealing with differences and contradictions, and taking responsibility. The notion *mental* is used here in the broad sense of referring to "the person's meaning-constructive or meaning-organizational capacities." It is not just about "how one thinks," but "how one constructs experience more generally, including one's thinking, feeling, and social-relating" (Kegan, 1994, pp. 29, 32).

Navigating in social space

The importance of flexibility and mobility (in space and in mind) in the global economy and the information society is a theme that runs throughout many of the contributions to DeSeCo. Kegan (2001) summarizes these views in the previous DeSeCo volume: "The adult of the 21st century will need to be able to travel across a wide variety of contexts" (p. 192). Indeed, today's adults are expected to lead successful, responsible, and productive lives and to fulfill many different roles in society and throughout life; to understand and act in different contexts; and to meet the multiple challenges and demands of modern life.

What does navigating in social space or traveling across a variety of contexts imply? To start with, social space, context, or the environment is more than a surface. In the DeSeCo Project, we apprehend context as structured in multiple *social fields* (Bourdieu, 1980, 1982) that make up society. Perrenoud (2001) provides numerous examples of social fields, including parental relationships, culture, religion, health, consumption, education and training, work, media and information, and community. Over the course of their lives, today's individuals are involved in most, if not all, of these social fields.

Social fields are characterized by specific challenges and interests, different forms of capital (e.g., money, specific types of knowledge, recognition, networks, and relationships), and ongoing struggles among agents within the field to gain power and define the borders of the field. As such, social fields are somewhat analogous to games. Both social fields and games have players, challenges, rules, stakes, and recognized struggles. Thus, for individuals to be players and not just spectators, they need to acquire a familiarity with the "knowledge, values, rules, rites, codes, concepts, language, laws, institutions, and objects specific to the field in question" (Perrenoud, 2001, p. 130). In order to participate in games – or to navigate multiple important areas of life – individuals also need an awareness of the resemblance between demands that are specific to a game and those that are similar across games. At the forefront of navigation across fields and flexible adaptation to unfamiliar contexts is not so much "know that," but rather "know how," which implies, among other things, recognizing patterns already encountered in past experiences, establishing analogies between previously experienced situations and new ones, and using patterns to guide activity in the world (Canto-Sperber & Dupuy, 2001, pp. 81–82).

Dealing with differences and contradictions: Going beyond the either–or

Another frequently mentioned requirement in light of multiculturalism, pluralism, and postmodernism is dealing with differences and contradictions (Haste, 2001, pp. 105–108). One natural reaction to complex issues is to make them less complex, for example, by reducing problems and questions to sets of mutually exclusive alternatives or adopting hard-and-fast rules for dealing with differences and contradictions. However, such an approach is not only impractical in many ways, but it often impedes a holistic understanding of and interaction with the world. Our diverse world demands that we not rush to a single answer, to an *either–or* solution, but rather deal with tensions – for instance, between equality and freedom, autonomy and solidarity, efficiency and democratic processes, ecology and economic logic, diversity and universality, and innovation and continuity – by integrating seemingly contradictory or incompatible goals as aspects of the same reality. For example, the concept of sustainable development is one possible answer to the tension between economic growth, ecological constraints, and social cohesion, recognizing their complex and dynamic interplay instead of treating them as separate and unrelated, if not mutually exclusive, goals. Another example is the notion of the social embedding of individuals, a conception that counters the idea of the independent individual and is based on the assumption of a dialectical and dynamic relationship between the individual and society.

More generally, an integrated, holistic approach is most likely the best response to the often complex, intractable, dynamic, and multifaceted problems posed by modern life. Dealing with ambiguous or contradictory positions and actions is not, in itself, challenging. Indeed, most of us do so without thinking about it. The challenge – which must be reflected in key competencies – is dealing skillfully and reflectively with multiple, dynamic, and often conflicting aspects and recognizing that there may be more than one solution or solution method. As Haste (2001) argues, "As we recognize the need for a more complex picture of the world, the competence required is the ability to manage diversity and dissonance in a creative and coping way, and avoid premature closure or dissolution into relativism." Thus, individuals have to learn to think and act in a more integrated way, taking into account the manifold interconnections and interrelations between – at times, only superficially – contradictory or incompatible ideas, logics, and positions.

Taking responsibility

In the DeSeCo Project, "it is not any competent individual that is being imagined, but at the very least one able to function successfully in the liberal democracies and capitalist economic regimes that characterize the OECD nations" (Carson, 2001, p. 39). Today, in most OECD countries, value is placed on entrepreneurship and personal responsibility. Not only are individuals expected to be adaptive, but also innovative, creative, self-directed, and self-motivated and, thus, able to take responsibility for their decisions and actions in multiple social fields – be it as parent, partner, employee or employer, citizen, student, or consumer.

Throughout many of the contributions to DeSeCo appears the notion that individuals are expected not to simply follow what they have been taught or told, but to "think for themselves" (as an expression of moral and intellectual maturity), to construct their own knowledge and guidelines for action.

As summarized by Kegan (2001):

> *Haste, Perrenoud, Canto-Sperber and Dupuy, and Levy and Murnane all present us a picture of socializing processes, but they all ask "competent adults" to be simultaneously mindful of them (thus not a sociopath or irresponsible ward of society) without being captive of them (thus not merely a faithful, loyal, obedient part of an unquestioned set of arrangements).* (p. 199)

Taking responsibility implies that individuals – in order to meet the various claims placed on them – need to take a critical stance and be willing "to question much that…has been taken for granted" (Canto-Sperber & Dupuy, 2001, pp. 84–85), and thus "to take the socializing press as 'object', something that can be reflected upon, decided about, at times, but reframed"

(Kegan, 2001, p. 199). It involves, for instance, questions (Canto-Sperber & Dupuy) such as "How should I live?", "What should I do in this concrete situation, given my overall view of what a good life should be?", "Was I right to do that?", "Knowing the consequences of what I did, should I have done it?" and "Why did I take this path to reach this aim?" Thus, "responsibility is about being the originator of one's own perspective, about taking possession of it, and moderating it to one's own goal" (Haste, 2001, p. 115). This, however, does not pertain to an egoistic or individualistic conception of action – individuals are socially embedded. In fact, "the 'meaning' of something – including the meaning of our own identity and our own morality – depends on what is comprehensible and recognized within our social community" (Haste, p. 101).

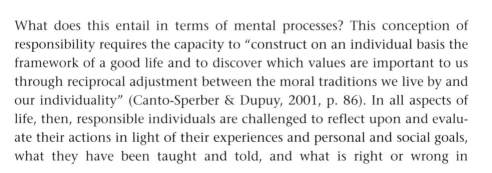

What does this entail in terms of mental processes? This conception of responsibility requires the capacity to "construct on an individual basis the framework of a good life and to discover which values are important to us through reciprocal adjustment between the moral traditions we live by and our individuality" (Canto-Sperber & Dupuy, 2001, p. 86). In all aspects of life, then, responsible individuals are challenged to reflect upon and evaluate their actions in light of their experiences and personal and social goals, what they have been taught and told, and what is right or wrong in conduct from the perspective of life as a whole" (Canto-Sperber & Dupuy, p. 86). This assumes an overall understanding of the meaning of things, actions, events, experiences, and critical values (see, in particular, Canto-Sperber & Dupuy, pp. 89–99; Haste, 2001, p. 101). This process of creating, extending, and applying meaning, knowledge, rules, and values reflectively is an underlying mental assumption of the many complex demands facing adults in various circumstances and situations.

Reflectivity – a mental prerequisite for key competencies

This higher level of mental complexity, as elucidated above, does not presuppose either a very high degree of cognitive skills or a high level of education, but "necessitates an overall development of critical thinking and reflective practice which has to bear on the sum total of formal and informal knowledge and experience in life" (Perrenoud, 2001, pp. 145–147). Thus, this approach is not foremost a cognitive or intellectual question, but one that concerns complex action systems encompassing appropriate motivational, ethical, social, and behavioral components, along with cognitive and intellectual components (Canto-Sperber & Dupuy, 2001).[4] Research tells us that this level of mental complexity will not ordinarily be obtained until adulthood. Before individuals can distance themselves from "the socializing press," make independent judgments, and take responsibility for their actions, they need to be well socialized. This understanding is based on an evolutionary model of human development in which individuals incorporate higher levels of mental complexity into their thinking and actions (Kegan, 2001).

Reflectivity concerns the internal structure of a key competence and is an important transversal feature relevant to the conceptualization of demand- and action-oriented key competencies. Thus, in regard to the competence model outlined in chapter 2, this analysis allowed us to go a step further in specifying a critical aspect of the internal structure of key competencies.

---

[4] Canto-Sperber and Dupuy (2001) offer, in their contribution, a possible model for further conceptualization of the internal structure of a key competence in terms of perceptive, normative, cooperative, and narrative dimensions (though they use the term competence) as underlying conditions, or prerequisites, for action.

A three-fold categorization as a conceptual basis

The demand- and action-oriented approach to competencies adopted under the DeSeCo Project resulted in the articulation of three categories of competence-related demands common across fields: *interacting in socially heterogeneous groups, acting autonomously*, and *using tools interactively*. At the most basic level, living entails acting on one's own, using tools, and interacting with others. When combined with the level of mental complexity required by modern life (reflectivity), it seems plausible to posit that it is not sufficient merely to act, but that one must act in a reflective and responsible way, that is, *autonomously*. The same is true for using tools and interacting with others; all three activities require a reflective approach to life, which is expressed in the titles of the categories. It is not sufficient to use a tool, one must use it *interactively*, and it is not sufficient to interact with others, one must interact with others in *socially heterogeneous* groups.

The conceptualization of the three categories of key competencies relies to a great extent on the abstractions and theorizations of the scholars that contributed to DeSeCo. For instance, "the ability to join, form, and function effectively in social groups" is advanced by Cecilia Ridgeway (2001, p. 206) as "the one truly universal key competency." The concept of the "autonomous actor" is a main focus of Perrenoud's essay (2001). And the "tool user" model is developed by Haste (2001). Although these concepts and models are prominently elaborated in those particular essays, many of the same features are found in other contributions, albeit often with a different emphasis. Our understanding is that these concepts and the underlying theoretical models and arguments put forth by the scholars are relevant across the disciplinary perspectives and, thus, have transdisciplinary character. Naturally, some concepts were further elaborated, adapted, and assimilated in light of the many exchanges that took place in the course of the work.

Conceptual elements or models that proved to be particularly relevant for the construction of the three categories include understanding the relationship between the individual and society as dialectical and dynamic; the notion of tools (in the broadest sense of the term) as instrumental for an active dialogue between the individual and the environment; comprehension of the environment as structured by social fields; the evolutionary model of mental development underpinning the notion of reflectivity; and the necessary adaptation processes implied by the concept of key competence.

The three categories of key competencies are interrelated, yet conceptually distinct, abstractions. They are "ideal types" in the Weberian sense, and thereby provide a conceptual basis or tool for describing and mapping all potential key competencies and for increasing the explanatory power of key competencies by conceptually linking them to a broader theoretical foundation. Each of the constructs has a specific focus. The category interacting in socially heterogeneous groups emphasizes the individual's interaction with others. The focus of acting autonomously is on relative autonomy and identity. And using tools interactively concerns an individual's interaction with the world through physical and socio-cultural tools (including language and the traditional academic disciplines.) The three categories of key competencies (and each of the identified key competencies within these categories) imply the development of a higher level of mental complexity as a condition for competent and successful action in modern life. Acting autonomously assumes the mental processes necessary to navigate in social space with all that such navigation entails, to deal with diversity, and to take responsibility. The same is true for using tools interactively and interacting in socially heterogeneous groups. As theory-based constructs, the three categories form the basis for constructing competencies that empower individuals to play an active, responsible part in all relevant social fields.

The next section of the chapter elaborates on the three-fold categorization and puts forth, within this categorization, a set of key competencies. The key competencies identified, along with the categories in which they fall, are embedded within a normative frame in which democracy and respect for human rights and sustainable development are considered core values. They apply to multiple areas of life (understood as social fields in the sense of Bourdieu) and across national boundaries. And, as detailed in this section, they imply the development of a critical stance and a reflective approach to cope with the varied and complex demands of modern life.

Three categories of key competencies

The construction of the three categories and the identification of particular key competencies within these categories followed different, though complementary, paths. As discussed in the previous section, the categories of key competencies were constructed by way of a deductive approach based mainly on the initial scholarly inputs and the subsequent interdisciplinary reflection. In contrast, the key competencies highlighted within the three categories are the result of an examination of the many lists devised throughout the project in light of the established definitional, normative, and conceptual criteria.

What follows is an outline of the significant features of each of the three categories of key competencies, which, we emphasize, form an interdependent ensemble, and a brief sketch of the identified key competencies congruent with the conceptual basis provided by DeSeCo.[5]

Interacting in socially heterogeneous groups

In this category, the focus is on interaction with others. Through socialization and the development of interpersonal bonds, individuals are linked to the group, the society. In light of fragmentation and segmentation processes and increasing individual and social diversity and uncertainty, strengthening social cohesion and developing a sense of social awareness and responsibility are presented as important societal and political goals. Integration, networking, partnerships, solidarity, and cooperation are some of the key words frequently mentioned. There is a consensus among experts

---

[5] It is beyond the scope of this publication to thoroughly present and explain the detailed theoretical and conceptual background of the categorization of key competencies or to further conceptualize the particular key competencies identified. Our purpose here is only to shed light on select relevant features as time, reason, and expertise allow. What is important is to successfully explain the developed frame of reference for selecting key competencies and demonstrate that the categorization is meaningful within that normative framework and based on the conceptual work supplied by the numerous scholars and discussed with experts involved in fieldwork and practice. All interested parties are directed to the first DeSeCo collection (Rychen & Salganik, 2001) for a more nuanced and complete discussion of the concepts and theory-based models that led to and underpin the three-fold categorization. The volume provides a valuable resource and includes extensive bibliographies for the scholarship received from multiple disciplinary perspectives. As to the identified key competencies, they are only considered an initial sketch. We are aware that extensive literature exists on each of the themes evoked, and that further research and development are needed in these areas.

that in pluralistic, multicultural societies, in a world of different cultures, interests, values, and beliefs, it is necessary that individuals learn to join and function in groups and social orders whose members are from diverse backgrounds, that they successfully deal with differences and contradictions.

In the most general sense, competencies in this category are required for individuals to learn, live, and work with others. They address many of the features associated with terms such as "social competencies," "social skills," "intercultural competencies," or "soft skills" found in the submitted lists of key competencies. These terms designate, in one way or another, the ability to interact with other people, but often without clear distinction or definition.

Human beings are dependent throughout their lives on ties to others for material and psychological survival, a sense of self, identity, and social meaning (Ridgeway, 2001). Identity develops only in relation to and in dialogue with our surroundings, in interaction with others. Contact with other people is a part of human life; most of the time we depend on it. We live in a network of close relationships in which we cooperate, compete, and share (Canto-Sperber & Dupuy, 2001, p. 74). Thus, interacting in socially heterogeneous groups concerns the development of social bonds and coexistence with people whose backgrounds may be different from one's own, who do not necessarily speak the same language (literally or metaphorically) or share the same memories, history, culture, or socio-economic background.

The development of competencies related to this category is particularly relevant for creating social capital, networks of mutually reinforcing obligations, expectations, and information channels (OECD, 2001d). The following competencies are relevant for interacting reflectively and responsibly with other people:

- relating well to others;
- cooperating; and
- managing and resolving conflict.

The ability to relate well to others

This key competence allows individuals to initiate, maintain, and manage personal relationships with, for instance, a family member, friend, or neighbor. It assumes that one respects and appreciates the values, beliefs, cultures, and histories of others in order to create an environment where they feel welcome, are included, and thrive (Stein, 2000). This competence is also referred to in competence lists described in the DeSeCo country reports

(Trier, 2003). Finland's 1999 framework for evaluating educational out-comes includes, among elements of communication competence, "social and interactive skills" and "verbal and nonverbal perception and expres-sion." Norway's Core Curriculum for Primary, Secondary, and Adult Education lists two characteristics of "the spiritual human being": "the abil-ity to meet other cultures openly" and "respect and knowledge for other religions and faiths." Similarly, the U.S. Equipped for the Future project identifies "respecting others and valuing diversity" as a common activity one engages in as a citizen, family member, and worker (Stein 2003).

Relating well to others is not only a requirement for social cohesion but, increasingly, for economic success. Levy and Murnane (2001) point out that "both changes in firms and changes in the economy are placing increased emphasis on elements of 'emotional intelligence,' including the ability to relate well to other people." They go on to state that "increasingly, high wage jobs require not only mastery of cognitive skills, but also what econo-mists call soft skills, especially skills related to interacting well with other people" (p. 166). These skills are necessary for relating not only to fellow workers, but to clients and customers as well.

There are several prerequisites for relating well to others. Empathy is per-haps the most important, entailing taking the role of the other person, imagining the situation from his or her perspective (Ridgeway, 2001), and feeling what he or she feels (Goleman, 1996). It is "the ethical move par excellence" (Canto-Sperber & Dupuy, 2001, p. 87). Empathy leads to self-reflection, when, upon considering a wide range of opinions and beliefs, one recognizes that what one takes for granted in a situation is not neces-sarily shared by others. Another important aspect of relating well to others is dealing effectively with one's own emotions and inner mood. This abili-ty assumes self-awareness and effective interpretation of one's own and oth-ers' underlying affective and motivational states (Haste, 2001).

The ability to cooperate

Many demands and goals of modern life cannot be met by one individual alone but, instead, require those who share the same interests, purpose, or convictions to join forces in groups such as work teams, civic organizations, political parties, or trade unions. Thus, a second key competence within the category of interacting in socially heterogeneous groups is the ability to cooperate and work together with others for common purposes. There is broad consensus on the importance of this key competence, as the ability to work in groups or teams is mentioned as a key competence in almost all of the country reports (Trier, 2003).

Consistent with the definition of key competencies used in DeSeCo, the focus here is not on the competencies needed by the group as a collective, but the competencies needed by each member as an individual. Cooperating involves balancing commitment to the group and its norms with autonomous action, and balancing responsibility for active participation in the collective with the need to share leadership roles and support others. Important components of this competence include, at the outset, presenting one's ideas and listening to those of others, switching frames and approaching topics from different viewpoints, understanding one's specific role and responsibilities in relation to those of others and the overall goal, and limiting one's freedom and blending into the larger group. Once engaged in cooperative behavior, understanding the dynamics of the debate and the agendas and tendencies present, detecting the limits of solidarity and constructing tactical or sustainable alliances, and compromising between conflicting interests take center stage (Perrenoud, 2001, pp. 140–141). Finally, this competence entails negotiating and building agreements, and making decisions that allow for different shades of opinion.

The ability to manage and resolve conflict

A third competence is the ability to manage and resolve conflict, to negotiate conflicting interests and find acceptable solutions. Although there are occupations dedicated solely or in part to conflict resolution, such as magistrate, attorney, mediator, or ombudsman, all people face conflicts in their daily lives and must resolve them, usually without outside intervention. Conflict occurs in all aspects of life, whether in the home or workplace or in the larger community or society. It arises when two or more individuals or groups oppose one another because of divergent needs, goals, or values.

Conflict is part of social reality, an inherent part of human relationships, as the quid pro quo for liberty and pluralism (Perrenoud, 2001, p. 142). The key to approaching conflict in a constructive manner is to recognize it as a process to be managed and, thus, not seek to wholly avoid or eliminate it, but to deal with it in a sensible, fair, and efficient manner.

This competence assumes that individuals consider the needs and interests of others and recognize that it is preferable when all the parties involved in a conflict benefit to some degree (win-win solutions), rather than one party achieving all of its goals at the expense of the other parties. For individuals to take an active part in conflict management and resolution, they need to analyze the issues and interests at stake (e.g., power, recognition of merit, division of work, equity), the origins of the conflict, and the reasoning of all sides, and recognize that there are different possible positions. Other important components include initially identifying areas of agreement and disagreement, reframing the problem, and prioritizing needs and goals (what one is willing to give up and under what circumstances). This competence eventually requires recognizing when the needs and goals of others take precedence over yours, and generating options for resolving conflict in such a way that all the parties benefit (Stein, 2000).

Acting autonomously

Interacting in socially heterogeneous groups and acting autonomously have to be understood as two complementary facets of the same coin. Autonomy is a means of survival in groups and a key to equitable cooperation.

To be clear, acting autonomously is not synonymous with acting alone or independently. Acting and operating effectively in and on the world does not mean functioning in social isolation, nor does it necessarily mean acting solely in self-interest. We all play roles as "members of multiple communities, each of which offers us identity and personal meaning" (Haste, 2001, p. 101). In one's relationships with others, however, there is an important difference between orienting oneself based on the expectations of the other in the relationship, and orienting oneself using one's own criteria for fashioning the terms of the relationship. In the former, one is captive of one's relational orientation; in the latter, it is a vehicle for a form of connection, which one is autonomously driving.

Acting autonomously means that individuals are empowered to navigate in the social space and to manage their lives in meaningful and responsible ways by exercising control over their living and working conditions. Thus, acting autonomously means to act rather than to be acted upon, to shape rather than to be shaped, and to choose rather than to accept choices decided by others. Acting autonomously refers to participating effectively in the development of society, in its social, political, and economic institutions (e.g., to take part in decision processes), and functioning well in different spheres of life – in the workplace, in one's personal and family life, and in civil and political life.

To act autonomously incorporates two central interrelated ideas: defining oneself and developing a personal identity (including a value system) and exercising relative autonomy in the sense of deciding, choosing, and playing an active, reflective, and responsible part in a given context. Thus, individuals need competencies that enable and empower them to develop and express a sense of self, exercise rights, and take responsibilities as a citizen, worker, family member, learner, consumer and so on in the different spheres of life.

The image of an actor influencing relationships and outcomes is most commonly associated with the powerful, but key competencies related to acting autonomously are equally essential for those who are on the margins of, or who are discriminated against in, any social arrangement and for those who champion their cause. Both groups must be able to step back from the assumed, known, apparent, and accepted – the former in order to conceive their liberation, the latter to convert others to their position.

This category is compatible with a value system that promotes autonomy as an aspiration and basis for personal identity. Building relative autonomy goes hand in hand with the development of a personal identity (Perrenoud, 2001, p. 132). At times, however, the socialization process may work counter to the development of individual autonomy. Depending on the situation or context, this may happen for a variety of reasons, including a lack of value placed on autonomy (e.g., in the military, sects, or certain businesses), a clash of values (e.g., obedience, humility, or uniformity), or because autonomy is not associated with the status of newcomer. Autonomy is thus a matter of relative autonomy: making an individual as autonomous as possible within the limits of each organization or field (Perrenoud, pp. 145–146).

In general, autonomy requires an orientation toward the future and a meaningful life plan, and an awareness of one's environment, its functioning (i.e., an understanding of social dynamics and the specific challenges they imply), and the roles one plays and wants to play. It assumes the possession of a sound self-concept and the ability to translate needs and wants into acts of will: decision, choice, and action. This conception is diametrically opposed to a vision of the world in which individuals are forced to bury their identity in the collective and the established order (e.g., a totalitarian state).

Within this category, we propose the following competencies as relevant when it comes to acting autonomously in a responsible and reflective manner:

- acting within the big picture or the larger context;
- forming and conducting life plans and personal projects; and
- defending and asserting one's rights, interests, limits, and needs.

The ability to act within the "big picture"

This key competence involves understanding and considering the "big picture," that is, the larger – normative, socioeconomic, and/or historical – context of actions and decisions, how that context functions, one's position in it, the issues at stake, and the long-term and indirect consequences of one's actions, and taking these factors into account when acting. This idea is expressed to some extent by the slogan "think globally and act locally." Acting within the big picture requires and enables individuals to develop, construct, and maintain coherence in their actions and behavior.

In many cases, the big picture is the global system. In other cases, it is the society in which the individual lives or a specific social field, such as the community or the workplace. In any of these contexts, individuals must look beyond their immediate situation to the long-term and indirect effects of their actions, and beyond their own needs and interests to those of others around them.

This competence allows individuals to understand the issues at stake at a global level, their role and the consequences of their actions in a larger (historical, cultural, or environmental) context. In society, it helps to ensure that individuals act in a just and responsible way, even when doing so may require effort and sacrifice, be inconvenient, or have little immediate impact, or when the consequences for not doing so may seem minimal or nonexistent. There are numerous examples of such actions including voting, recycling, or purchasing "fair trade" products. In the workplace or in other collective undertakings, "big picture thinking and acting" motivates people by allowing them to value the contributions they make to the overall functioning and impact of the enterprise, even though their specific tasks and responsibilities are comparatively insignificant or the impact of that collective effort will not be felt until a later point in time, if at all.

This competence requires something similar to what Perrenoud (2001) describes as a "conceptual blueprint of the system of action" (p. 138). Expanding on this concept, component steps and skills of acting within the big picture may include:

- understanding the structures, culture, practices, and formal and informal rules and expectations of the system (Stein, 2000). This includes understanding laws and regulations, but also unwritten social norms, moral codes, manners, and protocol. It complements an understanding of one's rights with knowledge of the constraints of one's actions.

- determining the roles one plays within the system and the roles played by others. This involves identifying the direct and indirect consequences of one's actions and how one's actions relate to the actions of others.

- envisioning multiple courses of action along with their consequences and evaluating the various possibilities with respect to shared norms and goals; and

- monitoring the system, predicting changes, controlling the effects of actions to the best of one's ability, and readjusting forecasts and plans of action along the way (see Perrenoud, 2001, p. 137; Haste, 2001, p. 106).

The ability to form and conduct life plans and personal projects

The normative framework we describe recognizes that each of us has obligations, goals, and dreams – things we must, should, or want to accomplish. Examples include finding a new job, career, or apartment; retraining and learning new skills; traveling; and improving the local community or beyond. Each objective requires us to develop an idea or a plan for achieving it, whether that plan is informal and simple or formalized and detailed.

In focusing on specific projects and plans, it is important to recognize that they do not exist in isolation from one another. Our sense of identity and self-esteem is based on the continuity that we experience and create in our lives. We need to see our life as an organized narrative to give it meaning and purpose. This is particularly relevant in a changing environment, where often life is disrupted and fragmented (e.g., Sennett, 1998), and in the modern world, where tradition and absolute moral frameworks have lost much of their influence. As a result, not only do individuals need to construct plans for their personal projects and goals, but they also need to ensure that these plans make sense in their lives and are consistent with larger life plans.

This is not to suggest that individuals have to create their own mission statements and conduct a formal process of review for each project to ensure consistency with the larger design. Rather, when people create or are confronted with choices, their decisions ideally should be informed by their goals and obligations. For example, when considering a change in employment, one should consider factors such as alignment with personal skills and interests, the likelihood of providing income sufficient to support one's family and lifestyle, the availability of time required to acquire new skills, and consistency with long-term career goals.

The ability to form life plans and personal projects assumes an orientation toward the future, implying both optimism and potential. At the same time, it requires a firm grounding within the realm of the feasible, typified by identifying and evaluating the resources one has access to and the resources one needs (e.g., time, money, and other resources) and choosing appropriate means to actualize the project. It implies that one can prioritize goals and refine their meaning and use one's resources in an efficient and effective manner: in other words, balance one's resources to meet multiple needs, goals, and responsibilities. Establishing projects and plans also requires learning from past deeds, and taking account of future outcomes. The orientation toward the future must naturally be grounded in past actions and experiences. Once the project and strategy have been developed, monitoring the project's progress, adjusting where necessary, and evaluating its effectiveness become important activities.

Competence-based requirements similar and related to forming and conducting personal projects appear frequently in lists of key competencies. The country contribution process (Trier, 2003) revealed many such examples, typically phrased in terms of self-management and the ability to learn and work on one's own. These include "the ability to assess how new tasks can be tackled" and "assessing and analyzing one's own skills and learning processes and outcomes" (Finland), "self-directed learning" (Germany), "the ability to plan and organize one's own work and learning process" (Norway), "effective self-management" and "strategic competencies: (learning and working, planning, transfer of skills, elaboration, monitoring, perseverance, evaluation skills)" (Switzerland), and "allocat(ing) time, money, materials, space, and staff" and "creating and pursuing vision and goals" (the United States).

The ability to defend and assert one's rights, interests, limits, and needs

In order to have choices, meet needs, and assume responsibility, "one must constantly defend one's interest, rights, limits, and needs" (Perrenoud, 2001, p. 133). In our modern world, where individuals' rights, interests, and needs continually come into conflict with those of others, where individuals face increased responsibility for many important decisions and functions, and where the rules that govern these conflicts, decisions, and functions are increasingly complex, defending and asserting one's rights lie at the very heart of autonomous action. This competence is related to both self-oriented rights (e.g., the same salary for the same work) and needs (e.g., adequate health care), as well as the rights and needs of the individual as a member of the collective (e.g., actively participating in democratic institutions and in local and national political processes).

This competence is relevant in situations ranging from highly structured legal affairs to everyday instances that require assertiveness. People must use this competence both in public and in private, and when dealing with family, friends, employers, co-workers, teachers, neighbors, lawyers, doctors, corporations, service providers, and government.

The fact that the rights, interests, and needs of individuals are often established and protected via laws, contracts, and other official documents does not relieve individuals of the responsibility of acting on their own behalf.

In describing the law, Perrenoud (2001) emphasizes that it is "only a *resource*" (p. 131). It is up to individuals to identify and evaluate their rights, needs, and interests – through research, if necessary – and to actively assert or defend them. The development of this competence empowers individuals to assert both personal and collective rights, ensure a dignified existence, and gain more control over their lives. It means that individuals capably put themselves forward as a subject of whom account has to be taken, and adeptly assume their responsibilities and choices as a citizen, family member, consumer, and worker.

Using tools interactively

Using tools interactively represents the third category for key competencies. The word "tool" is used here in the broadest sense of the term, including both physical and socio-cultural tools. The social and professional demands of the global economy and modern society, the "information society," require mastery of such socio-cultural tools as language, information, and knowledge, as well as such physical tools as machines and computers. Competencies in this area are frequently mentioned in lists of key competencies, including those described in the DeSeCo country contribution process (CPP) and the supporting material developed for this project.

In using tools interactively, the adverb *interactively* is meaningful. In a world where individuals are expected to create and adapt knowledge and skills, simply having the technical skills to use a tool (e.g., read a text, use a computer mouse, etc.) is no longer sufficient. To use a tool interactively assumes a familiarity with the tool itself and an understanding of how the tool changes the way one can interact with the world and how the tool is used to accomplish broader goals. A "tool" is not just a passive mediator, but an instrumental part of "an active dialogue between the individual and the environment" (Haste, 2001, p. 96). It is a figurative and literal extension of the human body and mind.

The underlying idea is that we encounter our world through our tools. These encounters, in turn, shape how we make sense of and become competent in interacting with the world, how we deal with transformation and change, and how we respond to new long-term challenges. Thus, using tools interactively implies not only having tools and the technical skills required to use them, but an awareness of the new forms of interaction that can be established through the use of tools and the ability to adapt one's behavior accordingly in everyday life (Haste 2001).

The following competencies are relevant in this category:

- using language, symbols, and text interactively;
- using knowledge and information interactively; and
- using technology interactively.

The ability to use language, symbols, and text interactively

The focus is on the effective use of language skills (both spoken and written) and computation and other mathematical skills (e.g., via graphs, tables, and symbols in various forms) in multiple situations (e.g., in the family, the workplace, and civic life). It is an essential tool for functioning well in society and the workplace and participating in effective personal and social dialogues. This key competence could also be labeled "communication competence" or "literacies," but as with most such terms, their meanings vary widely or have no uniform definition, making such terms unattractive (see chapter 2).

An example of this key competence is reading literacy as defined in the Programme for International Student Assessment (PISA) reading literacy framework: "reading literacy is understanding, using, and reflecting on written texts, in order to *achieve one's goals*, to develop one's knowledge and potential, and to *participate in society*." Participation includes the "fulfillment of individual aspirations" in the workplace, in one's personal life, in social, political, and cultural life and "social, cultural, and political engagement." It further defines the extent of participation as possibly including "a critical stance, a step towards personal liberation, emancipation and empowerment" (OECD, 1999, pp. 20–21). Other examples of this competence are the concept of numeracy, or numerate behavior and mathematical literacy. As described in the Adult Literacy and Life Skills Survey (ALL) framework, numeracy involves not only the enabling knowledge and specific cognitive skills required to manage the mathematical demands of diverse situations effectively, but also encompasses the activation of a range of behaviors and processes (Gal, Tout, van Groenstijn, Schmidt, & Manley, 1999). Mathematical literacy, as described in PISA, is "the capacity to identify, to understand, and to engage in mathematics and make well-founded judgments about the role that mathematics plays, as needed for an individual's current and future private life, occupational life, social life with peers and relatives, and life as a constructive, concerned, and reflective citizen" (OECD, 1999, p. 12). A similarly broad, function-oriented description of writing or speaking literacy would include not only the technical aspects of using language correctly, but using it effectively to achieve a given purpose or goal.

Command of languages is naturally a crucial aspect of this competence. Mastering one's native language is seen as fundamental in all countries.

However, responses to the CCP indicate that there are substantial differences in the importance attributed to mastering foreign languages in order to meet the demands of modern life (Trier, 2003).

The ability to use knowledge and information interactively

The increasingly important worldwide economic role of the service and information sectors certifies knowledge and information competence as a key competence. Outside the workplace, information technologies provide individuals with improved access to material on almost any given topic, thereby enabling them to conduct extensive research and analysis on any decision made. To function successfully in all areas of life, individuals must not only access knowledge and information, they also need to use it in an effective, reflective, and responsible manner. For example, this competence is essential in such situations as researching and evaluating choices for products and services (e.g., education or legal assistance) and choices in elections and referenda.

A concrete illustration of this key competence is scientific literacy, defined in PISA as "the capacity to use scientific knowledge, to identify questions, and to draw evidence-based conclusions in order to understand and help make decisions about the natural world and the changes made to it through human activity" (OECD, 1999, p. 12).

Another example, taken from Norway's Core Curriculum for Primary, Secondary and Adult Education, describes the "liberally educated human being" as possessing a "sound foundation of knowledge and broad frames of reference; the ability to organize knowledge; methodological skills; respect for facts and sound argument;…the ability to acquire and attain new knowledge" (Trier, 2003).

This key competence concerns the ability to independently find and make sense of information and knowledge, without being dependent on others for that information. It assumes critical reflection on the nature of information itself, its technical infrastructure, and its social, cultural, and even ideological context and impact. Information competence is necessary as a basis for understanding options, forming opinions, making decisions, and taking informed and responsible actions.

Thus, using knowledge and information interactively implies a series of behaviors and dispositions, starting with recognizing and determining what is not known and identifying, locating, and accessing appropriate information sources (including assembling knowledge and information in cyberspace). Once sources are identified and information obtained, it is necessary to critically evaluate the quality, appropriateness, and value of that information, as well as its sources. Organizing the information (incorporating selected information into one's own knowledge base), using the information effectively to make informed decisions and take coherent action, and understanding – to some extent – the economic, legal, social, and ethical issues surrounding the use of information are other requirements associated with this competence.

The ability to use technology interactively

Advances in the field of technology – especially information and communication technology – place new demands on individuals in and outside the workplace. At the same time, they also present individuals with new opportunities to meet demands more effectively in new and different ways. In knowledge and information societies, this competence concerns information, communications, and computer technology. The importance of technological competence has also been emphasized in several of the country reports submitted in the CCP (Trier, 2003).

Technological competence, as defined in DeSeCo, involves more than technological proficiency. In many cases, new technologies are not difficult to master, especially if they are "user friendly" or represent modifications of existing technologies. Nor are high levels of technical skill or skills applicable to specific technologies always valued. Levy and Murnane (2001) point out that most high-wage firms do not require that candidates for entry-level positions possess knowledge of particular software programs. More important is "familiarity with the keyboard and a mouse, recognition that most software programs are put together the same way and have on-line help systems, and an openness to learning new programs" (p. 167). This implies the importance of adapting existing technological skills to new situations.

Although the ability to adapt to technologies is an important aspect of technological competence, its full power is only realized with an awareness of the new forms of action and interaction made possible by technology and the ability to take advantage of that potential in daily life. As Haste (2001) points out, it does not require much technical skill for individuals to use the Internet and electronic mail to complete tasks that are already part of their lives, such as corresponding with others or reviewing the day's news. That same technology, however, has the potential to transform the way people work (by reducing the importance of location), access information (by allowing instant access to a wide variety of sources and by providing a means of quickly sorting through large amounts of information), and interact with others (by facilitating the development of "virtual" communities of people from around the world who communicate electronically on a regular basis). Although individuals benefit from these transformations without going through the process of envisioning them or even thinking about them systematically, they realize the true potential of these transformations only when considering them in light of their own specific circumstances. It is, thus, the incorporation of new tools into common practice that gives people the familiarity with the tool, that allows them to adapt its potential to other needs, and eventually to accommodate their practices to that potential. As Haste (2001) remarks: "We cannot of course expect individuals…to anticipate the nature of such a transformation, but it is…a part of technological competence to be able to deal reflexively, in a coping manner, with such developments" (p. 103).

Understanding the potential of technology is essential in another, more common process of using technology interactively: identifying technological solutions to problems. In this process, one is not confronted with a new technology, but rather with a problem, such as the need to perform a task or perform it more efficiently. Thus, more important than technical proficiency is a general understanding of the purpose and functioning of different technologies and an ability to envision their potential.

Each key competence described here builds on a combination of cognitive and noncognitive aspects as defined by the nature of context-specific demands. Successfully managing those demands requires a critical stance and a reflective approach. It is important to reemphasize that none of the constructed key competencies assumes a very high degree of cognitive intelligence or a very high level of education. In Canto-Sperber and Dupuy's (2001) terms, action competencies – the underlying model of competence (see chapter 2) – "involve the psychological prerequisites for successful performance; they include problem-solving capacities and skills for critical thinking; they are forms of practical intelligence: the capacity to grasp the relevant characteristics of a problem and to select and employ a suitable strategy" (p. 76).

Key competencies in different contexts

The key competencies presented above are constructs and, thus, are in no way submitted as a final, ready-to-use set of key competencies. They are situated at a sufficiently high level of generality to provide a conceptual tool for thinking about how key competencies play out in different contexts, under different socio-economic conditions. What follows are some initial thoughts about the practical functioning of the key competencies, and about how to incorporate contextual variation into the framework.

The key competencies put forth within the three-fold categorization are conceived as necessary for a successful life and a well-functioning society. For example, reading literacy (as defined in the PISA literacy framework) – a specificity of the key competence "the ability to use language, symbols, and texts interactively" – is universally lauded, and, indeed, empirical studies confirm the importance of this competence for personal, social, and economic well-being. Obviously, though, this important key competence alone is not sufficient for coping with the manifold demands and challenges associated with securing an overall successful life and a well-functioning society. A more inclusive approach to the topic is necessary. The complexity of the demands and societal objectives in today's world calls for the mobilization of a range of key competencies; particular competencies are not sufficient.

The notion of *constellation* has been proposed to represent the interrelated nature of key competencies and their contextual specificity. The underlying assumption is that meeting any objective will require constellations, or interrelated combinations, of key competencies that vary with the respective context or situation in which they are applied. The central point is that cultural, situational, and other contextual factors that frame any given situation shape the specific nature of the demands that must be met. A constellation of key competencies, therefore, is a culturally and contextually specific instantiation of key competencies in response to the specific nature of the demands of the local situation. The specificities and relative weight attributed to key competencies within a constellation may be influenced, for instance, by the state of urbanization, cultural norms, property rights, technological access, social and power relations, consumption opportunities, and public order.

A graphical way to illustrate the relative importance of key competencies with regard to their contribution to desired outcomes in any given context is by conceptualizing a multidimensional space (for simplicity's sake, reduced to a three-dimensional space in figure 1 below), with each dimension representing the relevance of the respective competence to achieving the desired outcome in the context. Different contexts (country- or social field-specific) can then be located in the space depending on the relative importance of the contribution of each of the three categories of key competencies to the desired outcomes.

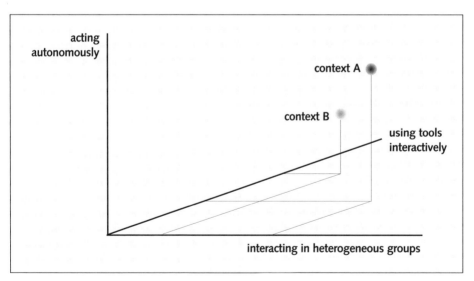

Figure 1: The relative importance of the three categories of key competencies in different contexts

Source: DeSeCo

Although DeSeCo was undertaken in the context of OECD countries, there is clearly a need for considerations of key competence to go beyond the industrialized world. Improving the quality of education, competence development, and lifelong learning strategies have become – in light of global challenges – important items on the political agenda for all countries, developing and transition as well as developed (e.g., Ouane, 2003; Riordan & Rosas, 2003; World Bank, 2002). There are at least three trends that support the hypothesis that DeSeCo's three-fold categorization is also a useful conceptual tool for developing and transition countries. First, the ongoing globalization and standardization process; second, the influences of international organizations, such as the World Bank, OECD, UNESCO, or ILO, which emphasize competence development and lifelong learning; and, lastly, the widespread adoption of a number of universal objectives, as expressed by the international conventions that form the normative basis for the competencies defined in DeSeCo. However, the extent to which these concepts have global validity or relevance is a topic that needs further research.

To conclude, the research conducted under the scope of the DeSeCo Project, incorporating scientific, practical, and policy-oriented analyses (Rychen & Salganik, 2001; international symposia in 1999 and 2002), provides the intellectual foundation for the concepts detailed in this chapter. From the initial research question – "What competencies are relevant for an individual to lead a successful and responsible life and for society to face the challenges of the present and future?" – a comprehensive conceptual frame of reference for key competencies has materialized. This frame is structured by overarching criteria that demand that any conception of key competencies be normatively and theoreticall grounded. A three-fold categorization of key competencies, incorporating the transversal notion of reflectivity, or a reflective, holistic practice, emerges from the theoretical inputs received. This categorization, in turn, allows for the extrapolation of particular key competencies based on empirical inputs. These key competencies, only an initial set, are conceptualized as forming constellations of key competencies, applicable to multiple social contexts in varying ways and definable in a multidimensional space. We are hopeful that the conceptual frame of reference for key competencies, while developed under an OECD-specific rationale, will be applicable to a wider array of nations, groups, and individuals seeking to effectively deal with the complex demands of modern life.

Chapter 4

Desired outcomes: A successful life and a well-functioning society

Heinz Gilomen

Introduction

The DeSeCo Project began by recognizing the long-term need for an over-arching theory-grounded framework for the definition and selection of competencies that could serve as a reference point for research, development, and interpretation of assessments and indicators. To date, the work has focused on developing the concepts of competence and key competence, constructing categories of key competencies, and identifying a number of key competencies within those categories that are considered relevant for all individuals in democratic and market-oriented societies. This work has been described in the preceding chapters.

The conceptual frame of reference and three-fold categorization of key competencies developed in DeSeCo have already gained widespread interest and support among relevant constituencies – policy-makers, researchers, representatives of various sectors, and international organizations beyond the OECD. At the same time, these concepts and related discussions suggest several strands for further exploration that, while beyond the scope of DeSeCo's original mandate, have the potential to lead to a longer term vision of enhanced international assessment and indicator systems and more effective government policies related to competence development and lifelong learning.

One area of particular relevance for further exploration is the relationship between key competencies and desired individual and societal outcomes. In the field of economics, the relationship between educational investments and economic performance in terms of productivity, economic growth, labor force participation, and earnings is systematically described in human capital theory. Developing a similar body of research to connect key competencies to the noneconomic dimensions of a successful life and a well-functioning society remains an important concern. "The non-economic returns to learning, in the form of enhanced personal well-being and greater social cohesion, are viewed by many as being as important as the impact on labour market earnings and economic growth" (OECD, 2001d, p. 17).

The question related to key competence, then, is: To what extent do key competencies actually contribute to a successful life and a well-functioning society? Or, more specifically: Which constellation of key competencies contributes to a given outcome, and to what degree? Answering these types of questions requires establishing conceptual linkages at the micro and macro levels between key competencies and the multiple aspects of personal and social well-being and validating them through empirical research. While this task is clearly beyond the scope of DeSeCo, it is possible to further specify the desired outcomes – *a successful life* and *a well-functioning society*.

This chapter begins with a review of the normative assertions and assumptions contained in various DeSeCo contributions regarding the notions of a successful life and a well-functioning society. It continues with a brief discussion related to quality-of-life research, followed by an outline of a number of critical dimensions that characterize a successful life and a well-functioning society. Clearly, the aim here is not to carry out a systematic literature review or a comprehensive analysis on this broad and complex topic. Instead, the goal is to tentatively define key dimensions of a successful life and a well-functioning society.

Competencies for what purpose?

"Education for what purpose?" has been and remains a central question, which, in the DeSeCo context, has been modified to "competencies for what purpose?" As specified in chapter 3, by definition, key competencies are competencies that contribute to highly valued individual and societal outcomes. This conception includes two important assumptions: that key competencies benefit both individuals and society and that they should contribute to something more than mere survival.

There is a consensus – at least at the level of discourse – that empowering individuals to envision and realize their own goals is an important outcome of education and, similarly, of the development of key competencies. Rekus, Hintz, and Ladenthin (1998), for example, claim that education should enable people to shape their lives in today's society according to their own aims. This includes "the fundamental claim...that each person is basically capable of universal self-determination and that at the same time he or she is determined to act accordingly" (p. 279). In a broad, interdisciplinary perspective, however, a primary or exclusive focus on individual outcomes would be too restrictive. This rather individualistic vision needs to be complemented by the societal dimension, defined by the needs and goals of society. DeSeCo's approach also goes beyond the view that key competencies are a "survival kit," a notion described, for instance, by the philosophers Canto-Sperber and Dupuy (2001) as "the set of basic skills and fundamental knowledge required for the survival of individuals or of democratic society and the continuation of community" (p. 76). Rather than considering individuals or society simply from the point of view of survival and continuation, DeSeCo has adopted the notions of a successful life and a well-functioning society, concepts that are much more dynamic as well as much more elusive.

In DeSeCo, depending on the disciplinary perspective, these notions are addressed in different ways. For instance, from a philosophical vantage point, Canto-Sperber and Dupuy (2001) list the following values as "necessary components of all good lives": accomplishment, the elements of human existence (including values of "autonomy, liberty, and humanity"), understanding (about "oneself and one's world"), enjoyment, and deep personal relations (pp. 74–75). The economists Levy and Murnane (2001) present "the economist's definition of a good life" as the maximization of income, but with limits on hours worked (p. 152). For Levy and Murnane, productive work is a foundation for broader goals, and they argue that the competencies they identify as important for earning a living coincide with those required to live a responsible and fulfilling life in a democratic society. At the same time, they caution that the economist's focus on markets and on the existing economy "implicitly accepts the existing distribution of income" (pp. 151–152). Although the other scholars have not addressed the topic so directly, the dimensions of a successful life and a well-functioning society can nevertheless be inferred from their discussions of key competencies. Perrenoud (2001), from a sociological perspective, associates a successful life with being able to "survive and live as well as possible, preserving…*autonomy* without infringing on that of others" and with not being "abused, alienated, dominated or exploited" (p. 126). And Ridgeway (2001) sees throughout the scholarly contributions a commitment to democratic, egalitarian societies, as opposed to societies that encourage the further development of an elite group of individuals.

Thus far, in DeSeCo's overarching frame of reference the desired individual and societal outcomes in terms of a successful life and a well-functioning society have been addressed only to the extent required to move forward with the conceptualization of key competencies. However broad some of the goals defined in international conventions (and referred to in chapter 3) may be, they provide a common starting and anchoring point for any further conceptualization and specification.

What is a successful life?

Some conceptual approaches

No single term is sufficiently comprehensive to convey all the aspects of desired outcomes for individuals. Elsewhere in DeSeCo, others have used the expression "the good life" (Canto-Sperber & Dupuy, 2001, p. 67; chapter 3). While this expression captures the normative dimension, which is an integral part of the definition of key competencies, it remains an ambiguous expression that can be interpreted either solely as a hedonistic quality of life or solely from a moral point of view. Although a successful life may be interpreted narrowly to mean a life characterized by the achievement of high financial or social status, it is open to a broader interpretation than the good life, as Levy and Murnane (2001) acknowledged in their contribution "Key Competencies Critical to Economic Success." Therefore, in describing highly valued individual outcomes, we use the expression *a successful life* in a broad sense that includes, but looks beyond, economic success and external recognition to consider a normative dimension and, as will be described later, the quality of one's life, in both objective and subjective terms. It is also important to acknowledge that although individuals' definitions of success may vary according to the basic thesis presented in DeSeCo there are certain constants (see, e.g., Canto-Sperber & Dupuy, 2001) that are valid for a vast majority of individuals.

One way of conceptualizing a successful life is to focus on the debate surrounding social monitoring and welfare concepts, including *welfare, quality of life, well-being,* and *living conditions.* In most societies, welfare is a political concept, the result of a consensus – albeit at a very abstract level – on individual and social conditions for which we all strive. Since such concepts are rarely formulated explicitly and in practical terms, we have explored a number of approaches for addressing this question. Heinz-Herbert Noll (2001) concluded that one of the main intentions underlying the debate on welfare in the social sciences is to identify the criteria that are used to define a "good life" as well as a "good society" in political discourse (p. 2). If living conditions are to be measured by these criteria in the form of a comparison of desired and actual conditions, they become the central components of research on social indicators and social monitoring.

Over the past 30 years, Wolfgang Zapf has developed a series of conceptual considerations on social reporting. In Zapf's opinion, welfare and its development represent the essence of modernization, with the term quality of life indicating a modern concept of welfare that was developed only in the late 1960s. In the second half of the 20th century, the quality of life played a central role as a target for social policy as well as a standard for social analysis and a frame of reference for assessing welfare (Zapf, 1993).

A famous example is the concept of the "Great Society," put forth in 1964 by U.S. President Lyndon B. Johnson. Noll (2001) describes Johnson's vision of the Great Society as being "concerned not with how much, but with how good – not with the quantity of goods but with the quality of their lives" (p. 4), thereby establishing as a goal the personal happiness of the American population. According to Noll, this represented a new concept of welfare that replaced the earlier idea that quality of life was synonymous with material wealth.

The inclusion of tangible and intangible, objective and subjective, and individual and collective elements marked a shift toward a multidimensional conceptualization of quality of life, a change also pointed out by Ronald Inglehart (1989). He noted a significant shift in values in Western society. While material well-being and physical security were once the most important elements, since the 1980s more emphasis has been placed on quality of life and postmodern values such as personal relationships, cultural issues, and environmental protection.

Habich and Noll (1994) distinguish between two poles within the multidimensional concept of quality of life: the Scandinavian resources approach and the American subjective quality-of-life approach (pp. 22–23). The Scandinavian approach is based on the concept of an "individual's command over, under given determinants, mobilizable resources, with whose help he/she can control and consciously direct his/her living conditions"

(Erikson, 1993, p. 72). In Robert Erikson's thesis, apart from income and wealth, resources include education, social relations, and mental and physical energy, which can all be used to individually shape one's own living conditions. This standpoint is, of course, intimately connected to the emphasis in Swedish society on collectivity and cooperation and the Swedish commitment to the idea of a welfare state.

In many respects, the resources approach is consistent with Amartya Sen's complex concept of capabilities (1987), although Sen places more emphasis on the mobilization of the resources than on the resources themselves:

> *In judging the well-being of the person, it would be premature to limit the analysis to the characteristics of goods possessed… In getting an idea of the well-being of the person, we clearly have to move on to the "functionings", to wit, what the person succeeds in doing with the commodities and characteristics at his or her command.*
> (p. 6)

Thus, a functioning is "an achievement of a person: what he or she manages to do or to be" (Sen, 1987, p. 7). This model of the relationship between resources, capabilities, and achievements appears to support the DeSeCo model of outcome-based competencies and provides a promising starting point for future efforts to explore the links between competencies and desired outcomes.

An alternative approach to the resources model is to define quality of life primarily from the subjective point of view. In this approach, the subjective well-being of individuals, as reflected by their satisfaction or happiness, is the predominant standard, regardless of objective living conditions. This has clear parallels with the perception of an American emphasis on individualism, where each individual pursues his or her path, regardless of background. It also relates to Noll's analysis of Johnson's Great Society, with its emphasis on satisfaction with one's life.

Erik Allardt's work (1993) contains elements of both a resources approach and a subjective approach. He developed a model based on three categories of basic needs: having (including the aspects of prosperity and material elements of quality of life), loving (interpersonal relationships and internal satisfaction), and being (activities as part of a community and for leisure purposes). Each category is composed of both resources for success and subjective considerations.

A similar approach, including both objective and subjective evaluations of success, is used in the German social reporting (Zapf, 1984). Figure 1 offers a conceptual overview of this approach, illustrating the interaction between objective living conditions and subjective well-being. *Well-being* constitutes the desired condition for society, as well as for individuals: a state where both objective living conditions and subjective assessments of well-being are "good." People who are not happy in their situation despite enjoying good living conditions are said to be in a *dissonant* situation and constitute a first problem group. An *adaptation* situation, where subjective well-being is assessed as "good" despite bad living conditions, is also considered a problem; in this case there is a danger of withdrawal from society. Finally, the group in a *deprivation* situation represents the classical target group of social policy. This approach has proved to be useful for the further structuring and application of the concepts in a political context, facilitating, for instance, the identification of at-risk groups.

Objective living conditions	Subjective well-being	
	Good	Bad
Good	**WELL-BEING** The desired condition	**DISSONANCE** The dilemma of dissatisfaction Potential for protest and change
Bad	**ADAPTATION** Paradoxical satisfaction: helplessness and social withdrawal	**DEPRIVATION** Classical target group for social policy

Figure 1: Typology of welfare position

Source: Zapf (1984)

Noll (2001, p. 13) points out that although comprehensive approaches to describing quality of life date from the 1960s and 1970s, they have lost none of their relevance. More recent approaches have not brought any important conceptual developments, but rather have highlighted specific aspects – in response to the need for more targeted social policy – and have, among other things, attempted to integrate the individual level of well-being with societal aspects. Sustainability, cohesion, exclusion, and human and social capital are the keywords in this respect. In order to achieve our aim, which is to establish possible reference dimensions for the normative category of a successful life, comprehensive concepts of welfare are evidently more useful than specific aspects.

The structure of the quality of life

The structure of personal well-being and quality of life has been examined from different points of view. One is that a good quality of life results from the maximum number of human needs being met. The best known theory of the relationship between different needs was put forward by Abraham Maslow (1954). He claimed that certain needs develop only when others are already satisfied. His theory thus led to a hierarchy of needs, which progress from individual physical survival through various forms of social interaction to an integrated and fully realized form of the individual.

Another quite different attempt to define a high quality of life for a whole society was made by the OECD in 1970. A list of desirable social conditions was identified by experts and political groups. The OECD's approach was based on social concerns, which were defined through a consensus process. The main theme here was that the social concerns themselves, or the needs reflected by them at a broad level, are the same regardless of culture. The more specific needs embodied in them, however, are of varying importance in different contexts, from the point of view of both their relevance and the way in which they are met (OECD, 1976, p. 8). Figure 2 presents a list of the eight social concerns published by the OECD in 1982.[1] These social

---

[1] The OECD is currently proposing a new categorization (Martin & Pearson, 2001; OECD, 2001c), which comprises three groups of social indicators: social context, social status, and societal response. These three categories differ somewhat from the pure PSR (pressure – status – response) model known in environmental research.

concerns – similar, at least in content, to the categories in many social indicator systems – provide a useful starting point for setting out the dimensions of a successful life.

Health	Education and learning
Employment and quality of working life	Time and leisure
Access to goods and services	Physical environment
Social environment	Personal safety

Figure 2: The OECD list of social concerns

Source: OECD (1982)

In addition, the concept of social field (see also chapter 3) and the capital approach as theorized by Pierre Bourdieu (1983) in "Forms of Capital" provide further theoretical underpinning for structuring and conceptualizing the dimensions of a successful life in terms of access and availability of resources. Bourdieu expands the notion of capital beyond its economic conception, which emphasizes material exchanges, to include "immaterial" and "noneconomic" forms of capital, specifically, cultural and social capital. In contrast to current descriptions of social capital that emphasize the benefits to society of networks with others (e.g., Putnam, 2001; Coleman, 1988), his focus is on the different and unequal ways in which individuals benefit. Cultural capital is associated with academic success. It includes "the ensemble of cultivated dispositions that are internalized by the individual through socialization and that constitute schemes of appreciation and understanding" (Swartz, 1997), material objects such as books and paintings, and institutionalized academic credentials. All three forms of capital can be acquired and exchanged in the ways commonly associated with economic capital. Possession or constitution of capital in the broadest sense is therefore critical for the materialization of success in different social fields.

The various approaches and concepts discussed in this section illustrate different yet complementary ways in which individual-level goals, needs, and prerequisites for success can be conceptualized, and thereby do shed light on the complexity of the topic.

Dimensions of a successful life

For our purpose – which is to initiate the discussion of what are some of the specific aspects of desired outcomes – the conceptual inputs outlined above provide rich source material for elucidating the critical dimensions of a successful life. Thus, it is against this backdrop of social concerns and concepts associated with access to and availability of resources that we put forth a set of eight principal dimensions of a successful life (figure 3).

Economic positions and resources

This dimension deals with the classical economic area, which undoubtedly belongs to the most elementary categories of highly valued outcomes, even in postindustrial society. There is hardly any other area of life that plays such a decisive role in social position, distribution of power, and quality of life as the economic dimension.

Resources in the form of income and wealth naturally fulfill a primary function of covering daily needs, but they affect other areas of life as well. In the form of high-value assets, they play a social role, indicating the social position of an individual, family, or group. Also, financial resources are an important factor in self-esteem, especially if they are acquired through highly respected activities, principally, gainful employment.

Access to gainful employment is closely connected to aspects of the use of power in critical social arenas. Those who fill the highest positions within the hierarchy of employment wield a considerable amount of power and influence over those with lower positions. In line with Helmut Schelsky (1972), Noll (1978, p. 210) refers to the psychological, economic, and social functions of gainful employment, which plays a decisive role in forming one's individual identity, is a major indication of one's social status, and provides for one's daily material needs through the acquisition of resources.

Economic positions and resources
  • gainful employment
  • income and wealth

Political rights and power
  • participation in political decisions
  • participation in interest groups

Intellectual resources
  • participation in formal education
  • availability of learning foundations

Housing and infrastructure
  • quality of housing
  • infrastructure of surrounding environment

Personal health and security
  • subjective and objective health
  • personal security

Social networks (social capital)
  • family and friends
  • relatives and acquaintances

Leisure and cultural activities
  • participation in leisure activities
  • participation in cultural activities

Personal satisfaction and value orientation
  • personal satisfaction
  • autonomy in value orientation

Figure 3: Principal dimensions of a successful life

Source: DeSeCo

The relevance of key competencies for both gainful employment and income and wealth is underpinned by human capital theory and by other theories regarding the relationship between educational attainment and earnings (such as signaling theory and principal-agent theory), as stated, for example, by Levy and Murnane (2001, pp. 154–155). Levy and Murnane's work has shown that success in the economic area occurs on a continuous scale of intensity and is influenced by an individual's possession of competencies.

Political rights and power

Political rights and participation in collective affairs constitute a basic dimension of democracy. But even if the principle of one (wo)man, one vote is applied in practice, the ways modern societies function provide different degrees of power-sharing. Participation in political decision-making often begins at the preparatory stage, and the formal processes of elections and voting are only highly specific forms of participation that offer very differentiated opportunities to influence events. Although political participation is a common item in surveys and social indicator systems, thereby making an implicit connection to influence, aspects of power are rarely addressed directly in the debate on welfare and quality of life.

Exercising power and taking part in political decision-making can take place through serving as an elected official at the national, regional, or local level. More commonly, however, individuals participate in the political process through their involvement with interest groups (such as trade unions, employers' associations, or political parties) or with citizens' movements. In his contribution to DeSeCo, Perrenoud (2001) raised the question of power, and associated successful life with relative autonomy. He defined competencies needed to "avoid being at the mercy of strategies and decisions adopted by the other actors" (p. 130). Access to influence and participation in collective affairs constitutes an important dimension of a successful life.

Intellectual resources

Apart from the economic dimension, education is the central factor that governs social status. In addition, Maslow (1971; Maslow & Lowery, 1998) posits that knowing, understanding, and exploring are major components of "self-realization." Others concur that intellectual resources are decisive preconditions for personal well-being (e.g., Vogel, Andersson, Davidsson, & Häll, 1988, p. 34).

Access to intellectual resources is important in two respects. First, it encompasses the topic of access to educational programs, in particular to higher education, the center of a classical debate regarding inequality and equity in education. Second, intellectual resources are relevant to the availability of key competencies. Although these two aspects – education and competence – are of course linked, the International Adult Literacy Survey (IALS) showed that they are not identical (OECD, Human Resources Development Canada, & Statistics Canada, 1997).

The acquisition of intellectual resources depends on certain preconditions. For example, participation and success in higher education and in continuing education seem to be dependent on previously acquired learning foundations and competencies. In this respect, we are thinking, in particular, of the ability to use cognitive tools interactively (see, in particular, chapter 3) in reference to Haste's (2001) "Tool User" model (p. 96).

Housing and infrastructure

Housing and the infrastructure of the surrounding environment are fundamental components of living conditions, falling into the most basic category of Maslow's hierarchy of needs and representing a basic pillar of welfare policy.

Here, housing refers specifically to the quality of one's dwelling, in the sense of its physical elements, such as the soundness of its structure, its ability to protect from severe weather conditions, the existence and functioning of major systems (e.g., plumbing, heating, and electric), and the sufficiency of its furnishings and appliances. Infrastructure of the surrounding environment refers to the quality of the community in terms of, for example, the level of pollution and the availability of the elements of a collective infrastructure, such as water and sewage, energy, telecommunications, roads, and public transportation.

Personal health and security

The absence of major physical handicaps, that is, the guarantee of physical integrity and activity, is also a fundamental category of quality of life. But this dimension extends beyond that narrow conception of health to the broader one employed by the World Health Organization (WHO, 1946): "Health is a state of complete physical, mental and social well-being and not merely the absence of disease or infirmity." It also includes the aspect of security – the guarantee of personal freedom from injury. Both aspects can be influenced by personal behavior and are thus reference dimensions for key competencies. This dimension is both an outright good for the individual and a prerequisite for other aspects of the quality of life.

Social networks

A solid foothold in social networks constitutes another important dimension of the quality of life. It is of the highest importance in all aspects of life – work, leisure, family, politics, etc. More recently, this dimension has been discussed as an aspect of the concept of social capital (Bourdieu, 1980; Coleman, 1988; OECD, 2001d; Putnam, 2001).

Social networks can exist at a highly personal level (family, friends), on a broader level (relatives, acquaintances), or as informal networks (clubs and interest groups). As will be described later, they are essential to a well-functioning society, but they are also included here as a dimension of a successful life because they can be mobilized for personal ends.

Leisure and cultural activities

Leisure and cultural activities are regarded as an essential dimension of living conditions (L'Hardy, Guével, & Soleilhavoup, 1996, p. 372). Bourdieu (1979) analyzed how leisure and cultural activities, among other things, are used to express and emphasize class distinction. Using numerous examples, Bourdieu showed how social groups subtly differentiate themselves from the classes beneath them through fine differences in consumption habits and gestures. Thus, from a sociological standpoint, culture and leisure are important aspects of social positioning, making access to leisure and culture a key dimension of a successful life.

Personal satisfaction and value orientation

We have already referred in various ways to the importance of personal satisfaction and value orientation as aspects of the quality of life. Since personal satisfaction and objective living conditions are not necessarily identical (see figure 1), personal satisfaction has its own significance in the discussion of success in life. Similarly, autonomy in value orientation is to a great extent independent of the availability of resources in the broader sense and of access to power, which is a key aspect of the other dimensions.

General remarks

These eight dimensions of a successful life represent critical elements of a possible frame of reference for conceptualizing the links between key competencies and desired outcomes, a potential follow-up activity to the DeSeCo Project. Such work will be essential not only for validating the key competencies identified, but also for providing evidence of the contributions of key competencies (other than basic skills) to economic success and expanding the analyses to examine their contributions to noneconomic outcomes.

Several important aspects of the ideas put forth here deserve particular mention. First, the notion of a successful life is a multidimensional concept incorporating objective and subjective elements of well-being. It includes not only outcomes in a strict sense, but elements that are more accurately described as *access* to and *availability* of resources, as well as the resources themselves.

Second, it should be emphasized that these dimensions are not of equal importance for every individual, for every context, and for all societies. The issues at stake on which they are based, however, are generally valid for democratic, developed societies. Thus, the underlying assumption is that an overall successful life, in whatever form, must always take into account all these dimensions, though the importance of a particular dimension may vary across contexts.

Finally, it should be noted that these dimensions form part of a continuum. As a rule, they can be determined on a "more-less" scale. Since competencies are also assumed to exist on continua of varying intensity, the dimensions of a successful life are ideally suited for analyzing empirical connections between key competencies and desired outcomes.

What is a well-functioning society?

Key competencies are defined as relevant at the societal as well as at the individual level. From the point of view of society, key competencies are of interest not only as determining factors for individual success in life, but also as a means of achieving societal aims. Since the organization of schooling and the transmission of basic skills and competencies have always been instrumental for achieving societal aims, we assume that these aims are a critical factor in the political debate on key competencies.

Discussions about the relevance of human capital in terms of competencies have focused to a great deal on their benefits at the individual level and their contribution to individual – mostly economic – success. This clearly represents, from the interdisciplinary perspective adopted in DeSeCo, an approach that is too individualistic and too limited.

If the topic is to be approached in a more inclusive and holistic way, it will be necessary to incorporate the societal perspective and specify the dimensions of a well-functioning society in a manner similar to the conceptualization of a successful life presented above. There is, of course, a great degree of overlap between the qualities of a successful life and those of a well-functioning society, since it is natural to expect that the conditions that create a well-functioning society also contribute to successful individual lives. But by their natures, societies must be far more concerned than individuals about institutional and structural aspects and issues of distribution, equity, and social justice, and a viable, sustainable future.

There already exist several examples of systems of indicators that describe the quality of societies, with varying methods and amounts of underlying developmental theorization and research, and go well beyond indicators of economic well-being to arrive at a broader, more complete picture of societal development that comprises, among other examples, social, environmental, and institutional aspects. For example, the U.N. Division for Sustainable Development (2003) has established a highly detailed system of indicators that address such themes as equity, educational level, international cooperation, biodiversity, economic performance, and communication infrastructure.

A systematic analysis of these and other indicator systems as a means of further specifying the dimensions of a well-functioning society and considering them in relation to key competencies would certainly be an interesting path to follow in the future. At this point, however, there is enough of a general consensus around several key features of quality societies – including economic performance, democratic processes, solidarity and social cohesion, human rights and peace, equity and absence of discrimination, and ecological sustainability – to suggest a set of dimensions of a well-functioning society. What follows, then, is an outline of a number of critical dimensions that characterize the quality of society and that are in line with the normative frame of reference presented in chapter 3.

Dimensions of a well-functioning society

Economic productivity

Economic competitiveness and productivity are major aims in all societies. Human capital theory describes a direct link between key competencies (acquired through investments in education) and access to gainful employment and resources (a major dimension of individual quality of life), the productivity of businesses and companies, and the economic performance of a society (see Levy & Murnane, 2001). Economic productivity thus constitutes a key element in the frame of reference for key competencies.

Democratic processes

Democratic processes represent a basic value in OECD countries and beyond. The principle that collective affairs should be dealt with by those people affected by them and that this should be done according to rules agreed upon by the community in advance is an undisputed social good. This principle is largely in agreement with John Rawls's (1972) conception of "just" societies. Most of the contributions to the DeSeCo Project are based on this tenet. Canto-Sperber and Dupuy (2001), for example, claim that

> *society is "well-ordered" when its basic social institutions are governed by principles of justice that everyone accepts and knows others accept. We assume, in addition, that the basic institutions of a democratic, just, and stable society are such that they induce its members to have a desire to act as the principles of justice require.*
> (pp. 71–72)

The participation of citizens in democratic processes is concordant with the dimension of individual quality of life that aims at participation in political decision-making and power. Barbara Fratczak-Rudnicka and Judith Torney-Purta (2003) point out that the true shaping of democracy is necessarily linked to the development and expansion of competencies in individuals. Therefore, key competencies are considered important resources that empower individuals to participate in democratic processes.

Solidarity and social cohesion

Solidarity is a dimension of social capital and is a fundamental element of societies. Noll (2001) refers in this context to Durkheim, who sees solidarity as a critical foundation for collective identity and social integration (p. 20). Solidarity is based on the components of shared values, which are established through individual value orientation. Strongly related to this idea, the concept of social cohesion also refers to the value system at the societal level. In addition, the concept of social cohesion includes the concept of common institutions. In this context, Dahrendorf, Field, Hayman, and Hutcheson (1995) speak of a framework of accepted values and institutions that characterize a society of inclusion (p. vii).

Human rights and peace

In presenting a perspective from UNESCO, Delors and Draxler (2001, p. 214) refer explicitly to the Universal Declaration of Human Rights (United Nations Organization, 1948), which was approved by the United Nations over 50 years ago. This declaration represents a clear system of fundamental orientations for global human and social development and a consensus across the most varied forms of society regarding an ideal for the quality of societies. Although abuses of human rights remain a major problem in many countries, the goal of human rights is developing a considerable normative influence. The Universal Declaration of Human Rights establishes the fundamental principles of human rights – understanding, tolerance, respect for fundamental freedoms – as central conditions for peace, and links them to education and competence development. The declaration states that

> *education shall be directed to the full development of the human personality and to the strengthening of respect for human rights and fundamental freedoms. It shall promote understanding, tolerance and friendship among all nations, racial or religious groups, and shall further the activities of the United Nations for the maintenance of peace.* (Article 26.2)

This statement continues the theme begun in the preamble that describes "recognition of the inherent dignity and of the equal and inalienable rights of all members of the human family" as "the foundation of freedom, justice and peace in the world" and suggests that the realization of human rights and peace is dependent on competence.

Equity, equality, and the absence of discrimination

Equal opportunities and justice are basic principles that are laid down in the constitutions of most modern societies and anchored in the Universal Declaration of Human Rights. There is no doubt that the principles are an aim that has not yet been achieved. In many countries, people still suffer discrimination in numerous social contexts for reasons of their origin or social position.

Along with Hutmacher, Cochrane, and Bottani (2001), we consider inequality to be the difference between advantages and disadvantages in material and symbolic resources. Such resources can be viewed as a combination of Bourdieu's (1983) forms of capital (i.e., economic, cultural, and social capital). If inequality and equality are combined with the normative ethical dimension of fair distribution and fair acquisition of advantages, we enter the field of equity. Discrimination can then be identified where there is systematic inequality, based on social or cultural background or social position, which cannot be justified according to ethical standards.

Justice, equal opportunities, and the absence of discrimination thus constitute an important dimension of a society's quality and serve as major reference dimensions for key competencies.

Ecological sustainability

Agenda 21, which was approved by the U.N. Conference on Environment and Development in Rio de Janeiro (UNCED, 1992), provided a visible forum for the issue of a sustainable heritage for humanity. The document draws attention to the contribution of ecological development and sustainable strategies to the economic and social fields:

> *Humanity stands at a defining moment in history. We are confronted with...the continuing deterioration of the ecosystems on which we depend for our well-being. However, integration of environment and development concerns and greater attention to them will lead to the fulfillment of basic needs, improved living standards for all, better protected and managed ecosystems and a safer, more prosperous future. No nation can achieve this on its own; but together we can – in a global partnership for sustainable development.* (Preamble)

To be sure, it is impossible to conceive of a quality society in which caring for natural resources and preserving them for future generations is not a key preoccupation. Ecological quality therefore means not only the absence of pollution and a high-quality natural environment today, but also the adoption and implementation of social strategies that ensure that future generations will also be able to enjoy a healthy environment.

Synchronization of the quality of life and of society

In most cases, the dimensions of a well-functioning society have analogues among the dimensions of a successful individual life. "Economic competitiveness and productivity," for example, identified as a dimension of a well-functioning society, is naturally linked at least to the individual-level dimension of "economic positions and resources" and possibly to "intellectual resources" as well. Similar connections can be observed between the societal dimensions of "democratic processes" and "solidarity and social cohesion" and the individual-level dimensions of "political rights and power" and "social networks." However, the dimensions of a well-function-ing society are not simply the aggregated results of individual pursuits of a successful life. Conflict is an inherent part of social reality, and, naturally, different goals and values at the individual and societal levels can come into conflict. For example, the methods and practices an individual chooses in order to attain and maintain a high standard of living may conflict with, among other things, the needs and rights of others or the health of the natural environment. Also, a well-functioning society requires a certain amount of efficiency in decision-making and administration, making it dif-ficult for all individuals to have a role in every decision or action that might affect them.

It is, however, our opinion that, in most cases, individual and collective aims *within* a given domain overlap. Trade-offs between different aims occur more frequently *between* different domains, both for the individual and the community: economic growth versus sustainable ecology and social justice, the availability of economic resources versus access to culture and leisure pursuits, and so on.

Sometimes it may be a question of perspective: Different goals coincide in a long-term, holistic perspective, but present a conflict over the short term. A similar thought, but with respect to key competencies and their utility, has been put forth by Delors and Draxler (2001):

> *There is a contradiction, which we see as only apparent, between the utilitarian, that is to say economically use-ful view of competencies on the one hand, and on the other, the view of competencies as being liberating forces enabling individuals to take charge of their own lives. That is where, it seems to us, it is more a question of time frames than of real conflict. Mere training for tasks can produce short-term results in terms of productivity, but the evidence shows that, in the long-run, economies are better served by a broadly educated population.* (pp. 215–216)

Ever-present tensions between various goals or values need not derail attempts to further define the relationships between key competencies and highly valued outcomes. In fact, these goals can be represented as constellations (similar to the way key competencies can be represented as constellations), which can vary both among different individuals and among societies. As a result, the form that constellations of key competencies take can be explained to a great extent by the dependence of societal and individual values or goals on context and culture, and by the relative importance attributed to the various dimensions of a successful life and a well-functioning society.

The distribution of different types of capital and of positions on the various dimensions of the quality of life and quality of society is what is at stake. Negotiating and balancing the interests of individuals with those of others and of society in general is of course a fundamental challenge to policymaking, the result of which ultimately depends on power relations and precedents in each situation. Power in its most general form is therefore an important transversal factor: For the individual, it consists of the ability to use or influence the functioning, structure, and distribution in each social field in such a way that they operate in one's favor in the important dimensions of a successful life, while the challenges for society consist of developing mechanisms that guarantee the respect for societal quality. The realization of both types of goals, those leading to a successful individual life and those supporting societal quality, is based on the availability of key competencies among the social actors.

In closing, we make no claims either in this chapter or elsewhere that DeSeCo has developed or will develop a definitive description of either a successful individual life or a well-functioning society. The goal here has been more limited: to identify an essential path for future research and to provide a start by identifying relevant theories and models and proposing critical dimensions of a successful life and of a well-functioning society.

Chapter 5

Reflections on international competence assessments

T. Scott Murray

Introduction

The purpose of this chapter is two-fold. It attempts to document the importance for policy-makers of measuring key competencies in a comparative framework at an international level. This is accomplished by drawing on lessons learned so far from international assessments, including the International Adult Literacy Survey (IALS), the Adult Literacy and Life Skills Survey (ALL), and the Programme for International Student Assessment (PISA).[1]

---

[1] In the past, studies of student achievement and adult literacy have followed different paths. Unlike previous comparative studies of students, however, PISA takes an approach similar to that used in IALS and now in ALL, building on explicit theories of task difficulty, rather than common curricular elements, as the basis for measurement. In contrast to IALS and ALL, which focus on the population of 16- to 64-year-olds, PISA seeks to profile the level and social distribution of reading literacy competence for a single age group of students near the end of compulsory schooling (15-year-olds). It also aims to shed light on the factors, both non-school and school related, that influence competence. In addition to reading literacy, PISA also assesses mathematical and scientific literacy. IALS assessed prose, document, and quantitative literacy; ALL is assessing prose and document literacy, numeracy, and analytical reasoning.

In addition, in light of DeSeCo, this chapter seeks to set out in pragmatic terms how the measurement of key competencies might be further expanded through international cooperation, including the development and administration of a new round of adult skill assessments using the methods pioneered in IALS. In doing so, it focuses on improvements that can be made and other challenges relating to key competencies that will need to be addressed if they are to be measured in a valid, reliable, and relevant way.

The policy yield of comparative assessments of competencies

The design and implementation of valid, reliable, and comparable assessments of key competencies at the international level are time-consuming, expensive, and risky endeavors. Not everyone is convinced that such assessments are worth the investment. One general criticism is that because the assessments are focused on policy development, and thus contain no mechanisms for feedback to individuals regarding their performance, they do little to help individuals. More specific criticisms come, for example, from officials of the French Ministry of National Education, who have argued that cultural bias in the measures developed for assessing reading competence precludes valid comparisons and who suggest that measurement in the additional domains identified by DeSeCo is likely to be even more unreliable (Emin, 2003). The approach to measurement taken in IALS has also been criticized by a group of researchers active in the adult literacy community, largely on moral and ethical grounds. They suggest that the models of proficiency underlying current assessment designs are inadequate because they do not capture the ability of low-skill individuals to accomplish tasks that typically require reading in nonstandard ways (see Street, 1999; Verhasselt, 2002). Similar criticisms have been directed at other assessments, including PISA.

Other critics have also questioned whether it is necessary to assess the competencies both of students at the end of compulsory schooling and of the adult population. Were competence a static commodity, then the PISA measures would suffice as a basis for analyzing and understanding the distribution of adult competence. Analyses of synthetic cohort data gathered for IALS suggest, however, that competence levels can change significantly over time, partly in response to economic and social demands for skills. Theory underpinning the key competencies identified in DeSeCo further rationalizes the need for assessments of adults: many competencies only develop during adulthood (see chapter 2). Although the dynamic processes of skill appreciation and depreciation in the years beyond initial schooling are not yet well understood, the preliminary evidence suggests that gains and losses are sufficiently large to be of interest to policy-makers and justify the expense of assessing the competencies of entire adult populations.

Although addressing these criticisms point by point is beyond the scope of this chapter, it is possible to counter them on a general level by describing the valuable contributions of these assessments. This section begins with a discussion of several important findings from IALS and then attempts to justify the investment required for improved future assessments by setting out, in summary form, what has been learned to date from comparative assessments of adult competence. In doing so, it draws on OECD publications (1992; 2001d) as well as on *Skill Development and Public Policy*, which was prepared to support the design of ALL (Giddings & Barr-Telford, 2000).

Policy benefits of an international approach

IALS was designed to respond to a particular set of policy concerns and priorities that remain relevant in both OECD and non-OECD countries today. At one level, the idea behind IALS was to demonstrate to economic policy-makers the central importance of education and learning across the life span. At another level, the study aimed to challenge the prevailing notion of literacy as dichotomous, a condition that one either has or does not have. The IALS data clearly demonstrate that when literacy is instead defined as a continuum, a range of social and economic outcomes can be associated with different levels of cognitive skill. The fact that the returns on higher levels of literacy do indeed increase beyond the point at which individuals might once have been considered literate demonstrates that literacy is an important concern for everyone, irrespective of skill level or level of economic and social development. Whether or not an individual's or a country's level of skill is adequate is another question, one that can only be judged in terms of the social and economic demands for that skill. This subtle change in orientation has transformed the nature of the public debate and has created a common purpose among policy-makers in developed and developing countries.

More specifically, IALS was created to identify the level and distribution of literacy skills in a heterogeneous group of countries, to shed light on the social and economic factors that appear to influence the level and distribution of observed skill within and among countries, and to render clear the individual economic consequences that are associated with skill at various ages and life stages. Aggregated to the macroeconomic level, IALS aimed to improve our understanding of the relative importance of literacy skill to rates of economic development, productivity growth, and technical innovation and to identify areas where literacy skill deficits might constitute a barrier to optimal performance in these three areas. IALS also sought to demonstrate the degree to which low literacy skill served as a barrier to the full and equitable participation of particular subgroups in national populations.

Analysis of the IALS data confirms that literacy skill plays an important role in OECD labor markets, conferring significant benefits over a range of outcomes, including the incidence of employment, the duration and stability of employment, the incidence and duration of unemployment, wage rates, and the incidence of receipt of social transfers such as welfare payments. Of these, from an economic perspective, the wage results are perhaps the most interesting, with literacy accounting for up to 33 percent of explained wage variance in several countries (OECD & Statistics Canada, 1995; OECD, Human Resources Development Canada, & Statistics Canada, 1997; OECD & Statistics Canada, 2000; Osberg, 2000; Green & Riddell, 2001). Analysis also reveals that literacy skill exerts a significant influence on a range of learning outcomes, including the probabilities of dropping out of school and of completing tertiary studies and the incidence, duration, and probability of securing employer funding for participation in adult education and training (Tuijnman & Bouchard, 2001).

The international assessment of adult competencies that is currently in the field, ALL, has the same basic objectives as IALS. Most importantly, by measuring prose and document literacy on identical scales and identical populations nine years after IALS, ALL should improve our understanding of the rate at which skill distributions evolve and what social and economic factors seem to underlie change. ALL also has been designed to improve the policy yield in four additional ways.

First, a new domain is being assessed. Direct measures of the analytical reasoning dimension of problem-solving skill have been added in an effort to determine whether this dimension captures some of the wage variance that remains unexplained by educational attainment, prose literacy, document literacy, and numeracy, or whether this dimension actually accounts for some of the observed wage variation that had already been explained by these other factors.

The inclusion of the analytical reasoning dimension of problem-solving skill in ALL raises important questions when considered in the context of DeSeCo. One such question concerns the degree to which problem-solving skill might, in fact, be a component or mental prerequisite of any key competence, and thus transcend the other measured domains. For example, the prose literacy domain might simply be considered as a class of problems that requires the reading of connected discourse to identify problems, search for possible solutions, evaluate possible solutions, and so on. Thus, reading literacy, numeracy, and other key competencies, such as speaking and listening, might be thought of simply as tools to be brought to bear on particular classes of problems. Extending this logic, any number of tools might serve a particular purpose, such as making an informed decision, but a particular tool, such as the Internet, might provide a much more efficient means than others for solving the "problem" at hand.

Although ALL was designed to explore the degree to which skill in one domain might depend on skill in other domains, most assessment tasks in all domains require some amount of reading. Thus, the ALL assessment is unable to detect problem-solving skill or numeracy skill in respondents with very low levels of reading ability. This is not a problem when viewed from an educational perspective, as one would want to teach the individual in question to read.

Second, the framework and associated measures of quantitative literacy that were employed in IALS have undergone extensive refinement for ALL, in order to yield estimates of numeracy that will be more easily interpretable in mathematical terms and less dependent on reading skill.

Third, an attempt has been made to incorporate a broader range of outcome measures. While IALS focused mainly on educational attainment and economic outcomes, ALL has been expanded to include measures of health status and social engagement, as well.

Finally, the background questionnaire administered to ALL respondents includes a module on familiarity with and use of information and communication technology and improved measures of unit wage rates. The ALL background questionnaire also incorporates an array of questions designed to capture the actual use of prose literacy, document literacy, and numeracy, at work and at home, as measures of the social and economic demands for skill faced by the individual. These questions are based upon research that suggests that skill use can be defined in five dimensions:

- *incidence*:   whether or not one uses the skill;
- *frequency*:   the number of times the skill is used in a given period;
- *range*:   the range of social situations or contexts within which the skill is put to use;
- *complexity*:   the level of mental complexity involved; and
- *criticality*:   how relevant successful application of the skill is to achieving desired or desirable social, economic, or cultural outcomes.

ALL restricts itself to measuring only the first three of these dimensions, as reliable measures of complexity and criticality have not yet been developed for use in a household survey context. However, future assessments need to focus on complexity and criticality because these aspects relate to important features of the key competencies identified by DeSeCo.

The ALL background questionnaire also incorporates a self-evaluation of the adequacy of skill levels in two dimensions: whether skill levels are adequate to meet the demands of daily life and whether they are a barrier to economic and social development.

Thus, data from adult skill assessments such as IALS and ALL can provide insights on a range of important economic and social policy issues that are not available from other sources.

Analytic benefits of an international approach

It is possible to make the case for undertaking international comparative assessments of adult competencies on the basis of the improvements they will bring in the richness of data and the resulting increase in analytic power. While the importance of considering competencies in light of broad societal objectives such as sustainable democratic development and personal well-being and thus the need to explore broader measures of success and well-being has been acknowledged (see OECD, 2001d; chapter 4), past and current assessments have focused mainly on the economic returns of competencies. From this perspective, the primary objective of assessing competence is to better understand how it influences the productivity of workers in labor markets, where productivity is measured by the wages earned at various skill levels. As noted by Heckman and Vytlacil (2000), identification of the true impact of skill or competence on the productivity of workers is constrained by a lack of variance in key variables. Specifically, current data sets do not yield sufficient numbers of observations in the tails of distributions, which would include highly skilled individuals with little education and poorly skilled individuals with high levels of education. Similar analyses of the IALS data by the author and others (e.g., Murray, 1995; Kerckhoff, Dietrich, & Brown, 2000) further demonstrate in several important ways both the overall benefits of international assessments and the need for data from countries that represent a wider variety of social and economic conditions.

Although most current analyses generally rely on measures of educational attainment as proxies for human capital or skill, it is clear they are very poor proxies in statistical terms, in that direct measures of skills identify significant numbers of individuals who possess more (or less) skill than their educational level would suggest. Analysis of the IALS data demonstrates that measures of educational attainment fail to capture large differences in skill attributable to differences in the level of skill acquired in youth (through differences in the quality of preschool experience and of education at the primary, secondary, and tertiary levels) and in adulthood (through processes of skill gain and loss). The data show that these differences vary significantly across countries, within countries, and over time.

Data from PISA and the IEA's Trends in Mathematics and Science Study (TIMSS)[2] reinforce this conclusion by revealing large variations in average performance and in the distribution of performance in what had previously been assumed to be a homogeneous group of developed countries, at least with respect to educational output. This implies that any analyses using educational attainment as a proxy for human capital will produce biased estimates and that the economic impact of skill on wages will be underestimated.

Further, analyses of the IALS data reveal large variations in the relative economic returns on skill from country to country. These differences can be interpreted as evidence that returns are attenuated (or amplified) by the relative conditions of supply and demand operating in a particular labor market. This seems to operate through three mechanisms – through initial selection (where credentials dominate as a screening device in conditions of excess skill supply); through higher promotion rates for workers with high skill levels (a positive effect); and through higher layoff rates for lower skilled employees (a negative effect). The classic example of the effect of supply and demand on economic returns on skill is seen in Sweden, the country that had the highest observed mean level of literacy skill in IALS, with a low level of variance around this mean. In Sweden, the wage return on literacy skill is very small. This does not imply that literacy skill is not economically important in the Swedish economy, rather that Swedish employers have a large supply of skill and find little difference upon which to differentially reward employees. The implication for assessment is that the sample of countries in any new assessment must contain a range of supply-and-demand conditions, specifically those where skill demand is high and supply is short, those where skill demand is weak and supply is strong, and those where supply and demand seem to be in rough equilibrium. Such heterogeneity can only be achieved through the inclusion of non-OECD countries.

---

[2] TIMSS measures mathematics and science achievement. TIMSS was administered in 1995 to 4th-grade, 8th-grade, and end-of-secondary-school students; in 1999 to 8th-grade students; and in 2003 to 4th- and 8th-grade students.

Pragmatic benefits of an international approach

The usefulness of an international comparative approach is also supported by pragmatic considerations. An international approach creates economies of scale that allow countries to afford access to state-of-the-art technology and to world-class institutions in the design and implementation of assessments. More specifically, international cooperation affords smaller and less affluent nations access to measurement technology and data that may otherwise be beyond their means. Finally, an international approach allows one to bring the collective research experience of participating countries to bear on the theory and practice of measurement. While such exchange can be time-consuming and occasionally contentious, the product is better and the findings are more readily accepted when such a collaborative effort is undertaken.

Building on DeSeCo in future assessments

DeSeCo was set up as a complementary effort to empirical studies such as ALL and PISA. Embedded in the OECD International Indicators of Education Systems (INES) Project, it was designed to frame what has been and is currently measured in international assessments and to provide conceptual foundations and guidelines for what might be measured in future assessments. Each of the current generation of international assessment programs – IALS/ALL, PISA, and TIMSS – draws upon specific bodies of literature to select and define what competencies are to be assessed, though in the future, the selection of competencies to assess can be informed by DeSeCo. The examples in the following paragraphs, which draw mainly on ALL, illustrate how DeSeCo's frame of reference could guide this process in the future.

ALL combined theoretical insights gleaned from the scientific literature on cognition and from occupational skill standards and job analyses to build an overarching framework to guide assessment, instrument development, and data interpretation (Binkley, Sternberg, Jones, & Nohara, 1999). The specific skill domains included in ALL furthermore had to meet four additional, more pragmatic criteria. First, the skill domain had to potentially influence a range of individual, social, and economic outcomes. Second, measurement had to be based upon a framework that defined the domain and identified the factors that underlie or predict the relative difficulty of tasks and, by extension, predict individual performance in a stable way in heterogeneous populations. Third, there had to be some evidence from previous research studies that valid and reliable measurement would be feasible in heterogeneous populations. Finally, there had to be an approach to assessment that would be sufficiently compact and efficient for it to be deployed within the context of a household survey.

One of the key conclusions reached through the DeSeCo Project with respect to current international assessment programs, including IALS/ALL, PISA, and TIMSS, is that what has been measured – despite having been selected in more isolated or project-specific processes – appears to have strong theoretical justification in the literature on key competencies. However, another key conclusion of DeSeCo suggests that frameworks and items in future assessments need to include tasks that require a higher level of mental complexity (i.e., critical thinking skills and a reflective, integrated approach; see chapter 3).

Many existing measures already appear likely to fall into DeSeCo's category of using tools (interactively). These include ALL's current measures of prose literacy, document literacy, numeracy, and problem-solving; PISA's measures of reading literacy, scientific literacy, and mathematical literacy; and TIMSS's measures of science and mathematics achievement. Of these assessments, however, ALL (and its predecessor, IALS) is the only one that provides estimates of the demand for competencies, of the social and economic import of the competencies that have been measured, and of the magnitude of advantage and disadvantage that is associated with various levels of proficiency in different life domains. PISA sheds light on the influence that school structure and organization have on observed levels of competence, and PISA-L (an optional longitudinal component added to PISA 2003) will reveal the extent to which competence influences postsecondary participation and completion rates and, ultimately, success in the labor market.

Canada and the United States are conducting a study to assess the component reading skills of individuals found to be reading at Level 1 (the lowest level) on the IALS/ALL prose and document literacy scales. While most assessments in the study will focus on components of reading, such as alphabetic awareness, word and number recognition, and receptive vocabulary, they will also assess speaking and listening skills.[3] If the proposed key competence of using language interactively is viewed as comprising reading, writing, speaking, and listening – although further exploration may lead to a different conceptualization – only writing will be unmeasured by existing assessments. Plans to measure skill in using information and communication technology in PISA and future cycles of adult assessment will further advance the coverage of assessment in the tool-using domain. However, further efforts are needed to represent the conceptualization behind reflectivity and using tools *interactively* (see Kegan, 2001; Haste, 2001; chapter 3).

DeSeCo uses three constructs to map and describe key competencies: interacting in socially heterogeneous groups, acting autonomously, and using

---

[3] This may address the criticisms from the adult literacy community, mentioned earlier, about the limited utility of international assessments for studying the lowest levels of literacy.

tools interactively. In doing so, DeSeCo acknowledges that these constructs incorporate multiple interrelated competencies, each of which, in turn, apart from cognitive components, also includes aspects such as attitudes, motivation, value orientation, and emotion. Coherent assessment programs, therefore, should seek to integrate and relate cognitive and noncognitive dimensions, which should be related to social, economic, and political contexts as well as to broadly defined outcomes.

In studies such as ALL, little attention is paid to noncognitive aspects; respondents are simply asked if their current levels of skill are sufficient to meet current or future demands. This is in keeping with the underlying economic perspective of the study: If skills can be shown independently to be of economic importance, social and economic forces will create the required incentives to make individuals value them or, alternatively, one will see signs of a market failure, a justification for government intervention. In fact, one of the most important uses of the IALS data was to convey the central importance of literacy to individual economic success, a key message in soliciting higher rates of participation in remedial education programs. With increased attention to competencies related to interacting in socially heterogeneous groups and acting autonomously, it may be possible to make similar statements about their importance for desired outcomes.

As noted above, coverage of competencies in the tool-using domain is comparatively good in the current generation of international comparative assessments. There is a fairly compelling body of evidence that supports the contention that these competencies have been measured in a valid, reliable, and, most importantly, comparable way. But internationally comparable measures do not currently exist in the other two domains. It is important that the goals of assessment in these new domains be translated into statistical terms to understand the nature and extent of the measurement challenge. From a broader perspective, the scope of future assessments has to go beyond the economic perspective and explore the relevance of competencies to the critical dimensions of a successful life and a well-functioning society, as outlined in chapter 4.

To do so, one first needs estimates of the level and distribution of competence in the population. Second, one needs to profile the social distribution of competence in order to understand its implications for policy. Third, assessments should shed light on the factors that underlie changes in the availability of competence to societies. Ideally, such understanding would flow from longitudinal studies. In the absence of longitudinal studies, repeated cross-sectional surveys can serve to monitor trends, including changes that can be attributed to improvements in the quality of education or educational expansion.

It is my (and others') belief, however, that measures of competencies related to interacting in socially heterogeneous groups (e.g., the ability to manage and solve conflict) and acting autonomously (e.g., the ability to form and conduct a personal project) will prove to be much more socially and culturally embedded, making comparative assessments much more difficult to develop than existing measures of using tools. It will require the investment of a significant amount of intellectual energy, financial resources, and time.

Experience with trying to develop internationally comparable measures of teamwork for ALL is instructive. Most researchers would judge teamwork to be an important manifestation of interacting in a socially heterogeneous group, largely, but not exclusively, in the workplace. Despite the fact that there is general consensus in the research literature about what constitutes teamwork and the factors that define proficiency, the ALL team was unable to derive instruments to meet the demanding standards set for the study. We trace this failure to the fact that teamwork attitudes and practices vary greatly both within and among countries. Also, it is important to note that the absence of outcome differentials related to teamwork at the individual level does not rule out differences at the level of firms, particularly in specific industries and with specific technologies of production.

The ALL framework document for teamwork (Baker, Horvath, Campion, Offermann, & Salas, 1999) defines a considerably larger number of factors that underlie and predict performance than simply being able to cooperate. The primary issue here is not a theoretical one, but one of measurement:

Whatever the theoretically defined constructs are, can they be reliably measured through observation or assessment at the individual level? The extensive development and testing of teamwork measures financed by the ALL consortium suggest that teamwork competence can only be observed *in situ*, through the observation of individuals interacting in teams, be they real situations, physical simulations, or computer-based simulations.

The PISA and IALS measures of competence have, by design, been administered at the individual level. In fact, both studies have gone to considerable lengths to preclude assistance from anyone during administration. The underlying idea is that these competencies are needed by everyone, and thus the studies' goals are to assess the respondent's ability to use a particular tool, be it reading literacy, mathematical literacy, numeracy, or some other domain, such as using information and knowledge, without the support of others, despite the fact that many such tasks are often solved collectively in real life.

Developing measures that reflect the new constructs will also be more difficult than might be imagined because the distinction between the three constructs is somewhat artificial, despite the fact that each has a specific focus. To illustrate, acting autonomously calls for individuals to play an active part in different spheres of life – in the workplace, the family, and civil and political life – and to manage their lives in meaningful ways by exercising control over their living and working conditions. Interaction in socially heterogeneous groups implies effective communication with others. Achieving these goals or acting in the desired manner often requires the use of tools, such as language, information, or technology. Therefore, competencies related to using tools interactively can also be thought of as important means by which competence can be achieved in the other two domains.

Policy-makers and other consumers of information on competencies desire to know more than their level and distribution in the population; they also wish to know their social and economic import for individuals and to know enough about their causes to develop remedial policies and programs. In particular, they want to know how competence in one domain is related to that in other domains. The design of studies to provide this information is complicated by the fact that proficiency in one domain can depend, to a significant extent, on proficiency in other domains. For example, it is difficult to imagine someone being able to cooperate or relate well to others in a modern workplace without being a reasonably proficient reader, speaker, and listener. Even where the domains can be conceived of as theoretically distinct, finding ways to measure such competence independently is difficult.[4]

The need to understand how competencies are related to one another creates some very practical difficulties. From a technical viewpoint, assessments of competence attempt to achieve two objectives: to obtain reliable estimates of the skills, attitudes, and other noncognitive aspects of individuals and to ensure broad coverage of the content domain of interest. International comparative assessments have generally adopted matrix designs that sacrifice the reliability of individual point estimates of proficiency for better coverage of the content domain for a given amount of testing time. The IALS experience suggests that a total average assessment duration of roughly 90 minutes is the maximum that respondents will tolerate in a household survey, whereas PISA suggests that school-based assessments of captive adolescents can be successfully stretched to three hours. Having to estimate both proficiency in each domain and the interdomain covariance matrix complicates matters further in that it increases the overall sample size and greatly increases the number of test booklets required in a balanced matrix design. For example, the sample requirement in IALS for three domains was 3,000 respondents and 7 test booklets. In ALL, for four domains, the requirements increased dramatically, to 5,300 respondents and a spiral assessment design involving 28 booklets. Thus, adding new domains to what is currently being assessed will pose both an operational and a financial challenge for participating countries. One solution to this

---

[4] A similar problem is observed with measuring numeracy and problem-solving (analytical reasoning) skills in ways that are unconstrained by individuals' ability to read. In ALL, the negative impact of poor reading skill on assessed numeracy skill was obviated by providing oral prompts to some questions that themselves place no reading demands on respondents. In contrast, the ALL problem-solving (analytical reasoning) assessment is heavily reading dependent, to the point where the test cannot discriminate good problem-solvers who also happen to be poor readers.

problem would be to conduct separate assessments for each new element that are linked through a common measure such as reading literacy.

Lessons from current assessment programs

Experience with IALS/ALL and PISA points to a number of additional improvements that would greatly enhance the quality and utility of the next generation of assessments seeking to incorporate DeSeCo's insights. These include the following:

Broadening the linguistic, geographic, and cultural representation of assessment items. The empirical evidence emerging from the psychometric and statistical analysis of the IALS and PISA data suggests that the attributes that underlie the difficulty of adult reading tasks are stable and predictable over a broad range of languages and cultures. This remarkable fact is crucial to the application of the IALS and PISA assessments in countries and languages not represented in the sample of assessment items used to establish proficiency. Were it not so, these assessments should only have been administered in the countries that contributed to the item pools. Nevertheless, even if unimportant to the scientific validity of the assessment, the geographic, linguistic, and cultural origin of test items contributes to the face validity of the test in these countries. Broadly representative item pools are also important in countries where there are large and diverse immigrant populations. For these reasons, future survey cycles should be far more systematic in seeking to achieve item pools that are, as much as possible, culturally, linguistically, and geographically representative at the global level.

Extending the Kirsch/Mosenthal grammar that underlies both the PISA and the ALL reading literacy measures to other languages. The IALS assessment was based on the groundbreaking insights of Kirsch and Mosenthal regarding the determinants of difficulty of adult reading tasks. Their theory, when applied to IALS and PISA, is capable of explaining fully 85 percent of item difficulty (Kirsch, 2001). Application of the Kirsch/Mosenthal grammar in the English language has provided a rich body of empirical evidence in support of the underlying theory, evidence that has been independently validated by the IALS and PISA data sets. To date, however, the Kirsch/Mosenthal grammar has only seen limited use in other languages.[5] Means should be sought to actively encourage linguists to apply and refine this work in their own languages, particularly at the lowest levels of proficiency.

As mentioned previously, some progress is being made toward this goal. The Level 1 study in Canada and the United States has expanded the Kirsch/Mosenthal grammar to include more traditional components or precursors of fluent, integrated reading in English, French, and Spanish. The ALL consortium is working in collaboration with the UNESCO Institute for Statistics and the World Bank to extend, refine, and adapt these measures for use in developing countries. The ALL design has also been expanded to include an "extended" core assessment for use in less educated populations found outside of the OECD countries, one that provides additional discrimination at Level 1 on the ALL prose, document, and numeracy scales.

---

[5] The author is only aware of two such applications, one by Jessiak in Polish and a second by a Dutch research team. Firmino da Costa and his team at the University of Lisbon have used the IALS framework to build a national adult assessment for Portugal. Isabel Infante and her colleagues have done similar work in six Latin American countries.

Analyzing trend data, which is crucial to setting policy priorities related to competence. The IALS data have demonstrated that literacy is not a static quantity that is acquired in standard quanta during initial schooling. Rather, observed literacy proficiency is conditioned by powerful social and economic forces operating throughout the life course, forces that can cause literacy to be gained and lost. For example, data for Canada indicate a secular decline in average proficiency beginning at the age of 45, a decline that is not observed in the Swedish population until later in life. These results could be the product of much more variable initial educational quality in Canada in older age cohorts or might reflect the impact of lower social and economic demand for literacy in Canada. Understanding which of these hypotheses holds true is of crucial importance to public policy. In the former case, the problem of low literacy will disappear as older cohorts age and die, whereas in the latter case, Canada will continue to "manufacture" low literates and all the related social and economic problems.

Unfortunately, IALS, being a single cross-sectional observation, was unable to shed light on this question. An understanding of such dynamic social processes is best gained through the observation of the same individuals over time longitudinally, as is planned in the PISA-L study. While highly desirable, large-scale longitudinal assessments of the competencies of entire adult populations are technically and operationally complex and expensive. Fortunately, repeated cross-sections can, by analyzing how changes in literacy are related to changes in underlying covariates, provide some of the same informational value as longitudinal data might. To enable such analysis, however, the literacy metric must be identical between the two observations. The Euroliteracy Project has already demonstrated that literacy ability is remarkably stable over a few years, at least in the four countries where respondents were reassessed. It is for this reason that the prose and document literacy measures used in ALL in 2003 are identical to those used by IALS and are designed to allow psychometric linkage of the scales at the item level. Two other studies currently under way may also shed light on the evolution of literacy skill in individuals. The first is a U.S. Department of Education longitudinal study of American workers, half of whom receive developmental literacy instruction. The second study involves the longitudinal follow-up of Canadian youth assessed in the first cycle of the PISA study. As noted above, an optional longitudinal component has been added to PISA 2003 (PISA-L).

Developing a better understanding of the social and economic demand for competence. The IALS data suggest that the economic demand for the utilization of skills leads to acquisition of additional skills or at least the maintenance of existing skill levels. Conversely, a low demand for skill may lead to skill loss. These market forces, however, do not always lead to the perfect balance between demand and supply, as analysis points to the existence of both skill deficits and significant skill surpluses (Krahn & Lowe, 1998). The costs of both are likely large: Skill deficits result in an inability to meet market demands, and surpluses indicate an inefficient use of resources (assuming that resources were required to impart and acquire the skills). These findings spark a call to explore how demand conditions the supply of skill, and also how it can fail to do so, particularly in the context of individual firms. This is especially important as leading representatives in the business sector agree that skill requirements of jobs are changing rapidly and that "in today's labor market, the creative and interpretative capabilities of individuals will increasingly tend to gain the upper hand" (Callieri, 2001, p. 228).

From a measurement perspective, and with a focus on economic outcomes, two lessons are implied. First, future survey cycles must include additional questions to determine how employees are called upon to use their skills: for instance, to explore not only the incidence and frequency, but also the criticality and complexity of behaviors over a range of skill domains. Second, a survey that assesses the skills of workers who have been selected from within a representative sample of firms is essential to understanding the links to productivity, interfirm variability in the demand and utilization of skill, and how these are influenced by the choice of technology. The expansion of this effort to other social groups and to other new fields will constitute an additional challenge.

Requiring extensive statistical quality assurance to ensure comparability. As noted in the IALS technical report (Murray, Kirsch, & Jenkins, 1998), considerable resources were devoted to assuring the validity, reliability, and comparability of data across countries. In the first cycle of data collection, most of these resources were directed toward the psychometric aspects of the study at the expense of the more mundane matters of sampling and data collection. Quality assurance in subsequent rounds attempted to redress this imbalance with some success (OECD & Statistics Canada, 2000). Such incremental improvement is crucial if international comparisons are to carry any significance. This goal is at the heart of the European Union's Euroliteracy Project (Carey, 1999) and of the panels of experts convened to provide advice and guidance regarding quality assurance in ALL and PISA.

It should be noted, however, that serious impediments exist to achieving marked improvements to quality. First, standard survey practices in many countries leave much to be desired. Second, the practice in many countries of subcontracting sampling and data collection to the lowest bidder often places serious restrictions on outgoing quality. Until countries are willing to invest more than minimal resources in these aspects of studies, there is little chance that quality will improve dramatically. Finally, it must be acknowledged that studies such as PISA and ALL are collegial undertakings with few meaningful sanctions for noncompliance to specified standards.

This is not a problem unique to these studies, but one that is faced by all international comparative studies involving sovereign nations.

The answer to the quality problem seems to lie in two areas. First, quality standards must be established a priori which, if broken, precipitate a number of consequences, including nonpublication and the identification and description of the problems in publications, typically accompanied by a separate or special presentation of the data. This was the approach pioneered in TIMSS and applied to the PISA assessment. On balance, the indications are that the approach seems to work. A note of caution is, however, warranted.

Consider the following experiences. France decided to withdraw its data from the initial IALS publication citing concerns about cultural bias, whereas the results for Sweden and Germany were published despite concerns over sample coverage and nonresponse bias in the estimates. Results for Italy were excluded from the 3rd IALS international comparative report due to concerns about sampling and nonresponse bias. Dutch results in PISA 2000 were not published due to fears of bias associated with low rates of school participation.

The linkage of the PISA and IALS scales through common items, however, provides a means to quantify the magnitude and direction of bias in proficiency estimates and, thus, to reflect on the adequacy of current quality assurance procedures and associated sanctions for noncompliance. For 19 of 22 countries, the IALS results for 16- to 25-year-olds were identical to those for 15-year-olds in PISA, including those for Netherlands and Italy. This suggests that their exclusion from publication was, in retrospect, unwarranted. If the PISA results are taken as the true value, then adult proficiency estimates in IALS for France appear to have been underestimated and those for Sweden and Germany overestimated. Given that the IALS items performed identically in both the PISA and the IALS studies, it would appear that cultural bias is not the issue. Rather, the observed biases can be attributed to problems in sampling and/or nonresponse error that remained uncorrected by the post-stratification and adjustment of weights.

These examples should not be interpreted as an argument against data standards. The real answer to the problem of quality – or, the second part of the answer – lies in the development and publication of a professional literature related to data quality, one that could serve to focus quality assurance resources more efficiently and to educate potential participants regarding risks and best practice.

Areas for future work

To date, DeSeCo has been largely a theoretical exercise. As such, it has raised important questions about the salience of what has been measured to date and has established a framework for thinking about priorities for future assessment.

The DeSeCo findings confirm that what has been measured at the international level to date indeed captures critical aspects of key competencies. DeSeCo has also raised questions about the interrelationships among key competencies, particularly about the degree to which performance might involve the deployment of multiple competencies. This question cannot be answered in the abstract but requires reference to empirical data. Thus, future DeSeCo work might concentrate on the analysis of covariance structures among the scales within PISA, ALL, and IALS.

DeSeCo might also serve as a mechanism to explore approaches to measurement in the domains of interacting in heterogeneous groups and acting autonomously. There are different possible starting points for beginning such explorations: using data collected on teamwork or tacit knowledge during a pilot study for ALL or data collected on self-regulated learning, which was an optional component in PISA 2000. In each case, the data sets can be used to provide insight into domains that appear to be considerably more culturally and contextually bound than the largely cognitive skills measured in the tool-using domain. A variety of small-scale, qualitative studies might serve as a means to move toward a large-scale comparative assessment.

To conclude this chapter, the DeSeCo process has served several important and related ends. One important accomplishment is that it has distilled a coherent and useful overarching framework for the assessment of key competencies out of a very broad survey of related scientific disciplines. Such a framework itself serves many purposes. It enables researchers in disparate and largely unconnected academic disciplines to discuss the issue of key competencies with a common rhetorical structure. It helps to guard against the risk associated with overinterpretation of what has been measured to date with, what theory suggests are, the entire range of key competencies, thus constituting a basis for situating domain-specific assessment frameworks and empirical results – particularly those from ALL and PISA – in a broader conceptual context. The DeSeCo framework also should assist in establishing priorities for assessment in future cycles of international comparative assessments.

Importantly, the DeSeCo Project also has served as a bridge between those involved in school-based assessments of key competencies and those assessing key competencies in adults, a bridge that is essential to both constituencies. Those involved with the development and implementation of school-based assessments need to know that what has been measured carries real-world adult consequences. Those involved with assessing the skills of adults need to know that educational systems have the means to teach the competencies in question.

Related, but more broadly, another lasting accomplishment of DeSeCo is that it has established a wide network of researchers with an interest in the issue of key competencies. Such a constituency can contribute to the substantive and sustained research that will be required to develop valid, reliable, comparable, and interpretable measurement technology for the entire range of key competencies identified in DeSeCo.

Chapter 6

Developing a long-term strategy for international assessments

Andreas Schleicher

Where do we stand today? *Looking back*

Are individuals in various social, occupational, and cultural contexts well prepared to meet the challenges of the future? Are they able to analyze, reason, and interact with the world through appropriate and effective methods and tools? Do they have the capacity to act autonomously and interact in socially heterogeneous groups? And how do these competencies contribute to a successful life and a well-functioning society? Various forms of large-scale assessments of the competencies of individuals have been developed or are planned in order to find answers to these questions:

- School-based assessments of competencies have contributed to assessing how effectively and equitably education systems function, what the key determinants of educational performance are, and how the delivery of education can be improved. School-based assessments have played a pivotal role in shifting the focus of policy and public attention from educational inputs to learning outcomes and by improving the public accountability of education systems.

- Surveys of adult competencies have extended this picture and made it possible to examine how knowledge and skills play out over the life cycle on various economic and social dimensions.

- Longitudinal studies are beginning to provide a means of assessing the extent to which the knowledge and competence acquired through initial education does, in fact, help to prepare young people for adulthood and the transition to work.

In addition to national assessments, comparative international assessments have been developed to enrich the picture gained at national levels by providing a larger context within which to interpret national results, showing countries their areas of relative strength and weakness, and establishing directions for national policy and instructional efforts to improve learning outcomes.

Whether assessments are national or international, important decisions and assumptions concerning the selection of competencies to be evaluated have to be made. Such decisions and assumptions are influenced both by considerations about the kind of competencies that are judged important in the respective contexts in which the assessments are undertaken as well as by various methodological and operational survey constraints.

A key difficulty for those utilizing and interpreting results from assessments remains, however, that the decisions and assumptions concerning the choice of assessment domains have often not been sufficiently transparent and, by implication, that limitations in the interpretation of results have often been disregarded (e.g., poor performance of students at a specific grade in an assessment of mathematics skills may sometimes have been equated with poor performance of the education system as a whole). Given the strong normative impact that assessments can have, the risk is that without recognition of their limitations, attention – and resources – in education systems will be diverted from outcomes that are important but that are not covered by the respective assessments. It is therefore important that the future development of assessments be guided by a better theoretical and conceptual basis for defining and selecting competencies. Such a conceptual framework can also be used to situate existing measures and to assess their validity.

The DeSeCo Project has, with the establishment of a conceptual frame of reference that includes the model of competence and three broad competence categories – interacting in socially heterogeneous groups, acting autonomously, and using tools interactively – makes an important first step in that direction. What remains to be done is to operationalize these competence categories and to elaborate implications for the development of assessment instruments. This chapter sets out an OECD perspective on some of the issues that will need to be considered in this process. While many of the issues addressed below apply at both the national and international levels, the focus of this chapter is on internationally comparative assessments.

Where do we need to be? *Looking forward*

In reference to DeSeCo's work on key competencies, what are the most important competencies for which OECD member countries seek internationally comparative measures and analysis? How should these competencies be operationalized so that they can be measured in a cross-culturally appropriate and statistically valid way?

Most international assessments to date have placed the emphasis on competencies that fall into the DeSeCo category of using tools. These include assessments of reading literacy, mathematics or science knowledge and skills (e.g., PISA, TIMSS, IALS, ALL), problem-solving skills (PISA), and civic education knowledge and skills (e.g., IEA Civic Education Study). Among the three DeSeCo categories, this is also the one in which most developmental work for future assessments is currently focused (such as the development of the instruments for assessing ICT literacy skills in PISA).

Some international assessments have begun to reach into the DeSeCo category of acting autonomously, such as the PISA assessment components on engagement and motivation, learning strategies, self-organized learning, and metacognition. However, these efforts are still far from satisfactory and have important limitations, given the nature of the tasks and the type of assessment instruments involved, which are essentially limited to assessing cognitive processes. The PISA effort to build a methodology that would establish ICT-based dynamic assessment situations may be a promising way forward but still needs considerable investment to mature.

Although the DeSeCo category of interacting in heterogeneous groups is generally considered important for the success of individuals and societies, methodological difficulties and considerations of cross-cultural validity have been a major barrier to progress in assessing competencies in this category. Small-scale attempts, such as the effort in PISA to measure self-perceptions in peer-relationships or cooperative learning, have not made enough progress to warrant pursuing such work on a larger scale. PISA is now giving consideration to assessing communication and cooperative skills, but significant conceptual and methodological work is required before assessments in this area become possible.

Given that many important aspects of competencies are not yet adequately covered in existing assessment instruments, it will remain important to progressively extend the scope of future assessments. This will involve advancing the technical measurement of competencies as well as improving the relevance and cross-cultural validity of the resulting measures.

However, where internationally comparative assessments are concerned, participating countries will need to consider the added value that they seek to obtain through international comparisons (as opposed to what can be achieved through national assessments) and address issues of the cross-cultural appropriateness and relevance of competencies and their measurement. The result of such considerations may well be that not all key competencies that were identified by DeSeCo will receive equal weight in future assessments, even if it were methodologically feasible to do so. Nevertheless, to conceptually clarify the coverage of existing and future assessments and to make their limitations more transparent, it is still useful to situate them systematically within the DeSeCo conceptual framework. This would also provide a basis for aligning the various international assessment efforts, for identifying gaps in coverage, and for guiding further developmental work aimed at improving the coverage of competencies in future assessments.

As relevant as improvements in the coverage of future assessments are, investments in this area need to be balanced against other dimensions where improvements in the development and use of assessments are needed. A key challenge, then, is to look beyond the expansion of the assessment domains and to address other dimensions, including:

The establishment of a longer term analytic agenda for future assessments, that is, a cycle of policy themes that these assessments would address across successive implementations. Measuring the quality of educational outcomes will increasingly lead to questions about the educational, social, and economic factors that contribute to improved education and learning and enhanced returns on investment in education in terms of personal, economic, and social well-being (see chapter 4). It would, therefore, be desirable to establish a cycle of strategic long-term public policy issues that could shape the analysis and reporting plans for future assessments. This would help to improve the dissemination of assessment results at the national and international levels, to make them more useful for supporting national development and analysis and, ultimately, to relate them more closely to teaching and learning processes.

A review of the target populations that future assessments will need to capture. While the development of school-based assessments and adult assessments is now on a promising track, there is a need for better information on key transitions within education systems and between education and employment, considering the growing awareness that competence development does not end at adolescence but continues throughout the adult years. To avoid an uncontrolled expansion of existing assessments, the assessment of new target populations would obviously require careful planning and an examination of how the various target populations would relate and interact and shape the analytic power and policy relevance of the respective instruments.

A review of the respondents from whom assessments will seek information. Closely related to the analytic agenda for future assessments will be to determine appropriate data sources. So far, the individuals assessed, whether students or adults, have been the main sources of contextual information for the analysis of results. Some contextual information has also been collected from schools or teachers, but with mixed success. Better insights into important individual, instructional, and contextual factors that influence learning and learning outcomes will require considerable investments. In the area of student assessments, observational information from teachers or parents might be considered. In the area of adult assessments, information about the work and life context could be relevant. Those responsible for the implementation of assessments may eventually decide not to pursue this avenue; that is, they might determine that other issues are of higher priority or that the technical barriers for collecting valid and reliable information from stakeholders and information sources other than the respondents themselves are too high. Nevertheless, it is important to make such choices consciously, on the basis of a coherent overall strategy, rather than in isolation.

Stronger links with qualitative information. Increasing attention is being paid to providing better linkages between comparative assessments and more targeted qualitative studies. The widespread interest in and utility of the video study of teachers carried out by the U.S. National Center for Education Statistics (Stigler, Gonzales, Kawanaka, Knoll, & Serrano, 1999) is an indication that the more in-depth, qualitative information that can be gained through means other than traditional surveys may become an important complement of assessment in the future. Such efforts can provide detailed information about teaching and learning, the quality of life in schools, or parental and student satisfaction that is beyond the reach of current assessment instruments.

A longer term strategy for the development of new assessment methods and the delivery of instruments. Existing international assessments have limited the collection of information to paper-and-pencil instruments, whether administered directly, as in the case of PISA or TIMSS, or indirectly through structured interviews, as in the case of IALS and ALL. Computer-delivered assessments have the potential to both broaden the range of assessment tasks and to establish dynamic assessment situations, thus tapping into new types of competencies and improving the authenticity of the assessments. They can currently be considered to be the most promising tracks for pursuing assessments in the DeSeCo categories of acting autonomously and interacting in socially heterogeneous groups. They also have the potential to significantly reduce the response burden for respondents by matching individual performance levels with the most appropriate tasks, thus avoiding situations where individuals are confronted with large numbers of tasks that are either too easy or too difficult for them, a problem that is usually encountered in paper-and-pencil assessments where performance standards vary significantly across countries and individuals. This is an area where methods are at an early stage of development, and their introduction will therefore likely be gradual and progressive and consequently require long-term planning across multiple survey cycles.

A review of the frequency of successive assessments. Many of the international assessments carry out successive assessments regularly. For example, TIMSS and PIRLS assessments are repeated every 4 years; the PISA assessment cycle spans 9 years, with limited updates every 3 years; and the assessment of adult competencies has been considered once during every decade. Considerations behind such assessment cycles have included balancing various resource considerations with the need to provide regular input into the policy debate and monitoring trends in performance standards of individuals, school systems, and countries over time. Little research, however, has been undertaken to evaluate the effectiveness and efficiency of these assessment cycles. The frequency of successive assessments should not be considered fixed, but may be one of the variables that countries wish to trade off against other objectives of the strategy. Perhaps most importantly, the different assessment cycles will need better coordination in the longer term. This does not merely imply better coordination of school-based assessments but, even more importantly, better coordination between school-based and adult competence assessments to build in synergies that have, so far, been left unexploited.

Over and above these issues, it will be critically important to continually assess the relationship between national and international assessment activities. Particularly in countries that have not yet established national assessments, there are at times unrealistic expectations as to what international assessments can achieve at the national level. It will therefore be important

- for international assessments to ensure that the focus remains on public policy issues that are not only high on national policy agendas, but where the international comparative perspective can offer important new insights. (Plans for future assessments should therefore be evaluated against the extent to which international comparative analysis provides sufficient added value to what can be done through national analysis and evaluation.)

- to recognize that there are multiple international organizations involved in the development and implementation of international assessments and, as far as the OECD is concerned, efforts should focus on where the OECD can make a unique and innovative contribution to national policy development.

- to recognize that international surveys are not necessarily the best answer to all questions relating to the development and impact of competencies, and to focus assessments on areas where they offer an appropriate methodology and have the potential to yield significant insights for analysis.

How can we get there? *Challenges and issues*

Because trade-offs may be necessary among many of the potential goals set out in the preceding section and because these goals involve high development and implementation costs, a clear direction is needed on what the priorities are and how they might best be achieved. This may require considerable negotiation among countries. An unbridled expansion of international assessments will make it difficult to finance and manage these activities and may detract from their effectiveness for policy. Some of the trade-offs that are involved include the following:

- Increasing the scope of assessment instruments in terms of the competencies to be covered may lower the depth of information obtained for any single assessment domain. In addition, for some of the assessment domains for which benchmarks are desirable from a policy perspective, reliable and comparable measures do not yet exist (e.g., for the assessment of interpersonal skills) or are prohibitively expensive for large-scale assessments.

- Placing a premium on the accuracy of skill measures, their cross-cultural validity, or their authenticity may divert response time and resources away from obtaining important contextual information (e.g., on individuals or their learning environment) that ultimately determines the analytic power of the instruments.

- There is also a tension between ensuring that surveys remain responsive to advances in theory and measurement and the need to ensure the coherence of assessments over time, which is required to establish reliable measures of trends.

- While increasing the number of target populations in a survey greatly enhances its analytic power, each additional target population adds significantly to the costs and complexity of the survey instruments.

- There may also be a tension between international comparability and the national relevance of assessment measures.

- The frequency with which assessments can be feasibly undertaken needs to be weighed against the use that is made of the results for policy development.

A strategy for setting priorities and weighing the respective trade-offs might lead through the following steps:

- First of all, agreement will be needed on the key policy dimensions that participating countries seek to address with international assessments, for example, issues related to the quality of learning as reflected in outcomes of learning systems, equity in educational opportunities, the adequacy and effectiveness of resource management, and the "durability" of knowledge and skills and their social and economic relevance.

- A next step would be the establishment of the policy levers that shape these policy objectives in the different contexts in which the assessments are applied. This, in turn, would require considerable research into developing analytical approaches to the ways in which the policy levers interact with the policy objectives.

- With a strong analytical underpinning, an assessment strategy and design can then be built in which different instruments coherently portray the various aspects of competence development and use in different age groups and social fields.

Some of these issues are discussed in more detail in the following sections.

How might a longer term analytic agenda take shape?

DeSeCo is providing a frame of reference for the measurement of competencies in relation to broad desired outcomes at the individual and societal levels (see chapter 4). As relevant as it is to know about the distribution of competencies among individuals, institutions, or countries, the interest among those sponsoring international assessments will increasingly shift to the individual and social consequences of this distribution of competencies as well as to the policy levers through which competencies can be strengthened and competence gaps can be mediated.

The value of international assessments for policy development will there-fore increasingly depend not just on the coverage of competence domains, but on the analysis of the results and how effectively these reach the actors in various settings, including policy-makers and analysts as well as researchers, school authorities, the business sector, and individuals directly responsible for the learning and teaching process. This is not only an issue of dissemination and public relations but also, and perhaps more impor-tantly, one of developing the right instruments to provide insight into important individual, instructional, and institutional factors that influence teaching and learning outcomes. Traditionally, the design and instrumen-tation of international assessments have been weak in this respect.

As an instrument that seeks to focus closely on public concerns in two broad domains – economic and social policy, including education policy – a future assessment strategy needs to progress in this respect and to yield clearer signals for

- evaluating different investments in competencies;
- informing policy-makers on how to improve the effectiveness of edu-cation and learning; and
- ensuring that relevant criteria for the successful evaluation of educa-tion and training systems are selected.

This could be achieved through the establishment of a cycle of strategic long-term education policy issues that would parallel the cycle of interna-tional assessments of competencies and that would shape the respective analysis and reporting plans. These are issues that are likely to challenge education systems in many countries in the longer term and where the potential for countries to learn from each other's experience is significant. Knowing that important policy issues will be addressed appropriately and in depth at some point in the future will also make it easier not to be tempted to address them poorly in the short term, a problem that all international assessments have encountered at some point.

Such a longer term agenda will also allow us to devote the necessary time to the development of measures of learning contexts, policies, and practices in some areas where this continues to prove difficult within the tight time frame of the implementation of a single survey cycle. Not least of all, it will allow us to focus resources for this on priority areas in each assessment cycle. Once appropriate measures have been developed in an area, the assessment strategy can then draw on them in successive survey cycles, as is currently the case for student performance measures, rather than replicating unsatisfactory background measures time after time.

At what age groups/populations should future instruments be targeted?

The DeSeCo framework postulates that competencies and their development interact with the life cycle of individuals. This needs to be reflected more systematically in a future assessment strategy. It raises questions about the age groups and target populations at which future assessments should be targeted. For example, should existing school-based assessments be extended to younger and/or older age groups? Should the development of a longitudinal assessment component be a future objective? How should the OECD assessment strategy incorporate the conceptual and organizational link between assessments of school systems and assessments of adult competencies? These are important questions that will critically influence the analytic power of future assessments.

While adding to the analytic potential, each additional target population will bring with it significant increases in costs at both national and international levels and thus needs to be carefully weighed to ensure that policy priorities and resources are well balanced. Pursuing all these avenues simultaneously is likely to yield poor returns and may make future assessments unmanageable. An appropriate basis for establishing priorities and consistent choices will be the establishment of an integral plan that shows how different target populations will feed into and strengthen the analytic power of the overall assessment strategy. That implies that future longitudinal and adult assessments should be built into the assessment strategy conceptually, even if they will eventually be pursued differently at the operational level. There is probably wide agreement among countries that the current focus of PISA on students toward the end of compulsory schooling should remain. At the same time, some countries have also indicated an interest in adding an assessment of children during the early years of primary education, not only to gain better insight into skill acquisition in the early school years, but also to obtain measures of growth between the primary-age cohort and the PISA population at the end of compulsory schooling.

Also, assessments at more advanced levels of education – including general and vocational programs at the upper secondary level of education and, indeed, tertiary education programs – have sometimes been identified as an area of policy interest, although assessments at these levels of education are largely unexplored territory.

A particularly important question that OECD member countries need to answer is whether and how a survey approach to the assessment of adult competencies should be undertaken within a governmental framework such as the OECD, building on the international experience of the ALL survey currently carried out under the leadership of Statistics Canada.

If agreement is reached that the next adult competencies assessment should become part of the overall OECD assessment strategy, new questions arise:

- Should one search for a comprehensive assessment of a broad range of adult competencies or is this an illusory goal, for example, because of differences in the relevance of skills in different age groups or different societal, cultural, or occupational contexts or simply for practical reasons and constraints?

- Should one choose, instead, a more targeted approach to assessing adult competencies and, if so, what would be an appropriate policy context and reference frame?

- Should there be a cycle of adult assessments across different age, occupational, or other types of target groups?

Other considerations, currently implemented in various countries as international and national options, relate to complementing age-based target populations – which are necessary in order to obtain internationally comparable assessment results – with grade-based components that allow results to be linked more closely to national institutional structures. This is an area that the future assessment strategy should seek to address more systematically as well in order to reap analytic benefits from such complements to the assessment strategy as a whole.

Some countries have shown an interest in extending student assessments with a longitudinal follow-up. The essence of longitudinal data is that the same people are surveyed on a regular basis over time. By surveying the same young people over time, it is possible to build an understanding of the changes taking place in their lives – and how previous achievements and experiences have influenced what is happening to them now.

The combination of a longitudinal school-to-work transition survey with school-based assessments provides an attractive potential for policy analysis: School-based assessments address issues relating to the degree to which students – in the case of PISA, those approaching the end of compulsory education – have acquired the knowledge and skills that are essential for full participation in society. A longitudinal survey would allow the examination of how the skills measured through school-based assessments play out in the transition from education to work and further education; the attitudes, aspirations, and behavior of youth entering the labor market; the economic and social benefits from participation in different forms of education and training; the patterns of transitions from initial education to subsequent education and training and the labor market; and the exploration of how access to postsecondary education and initial labor market success are conditioned by achievement, formal qualifications, and social origins. At the same time, while longitudinal surveys offer considerably more information value per unit of investment than repeated cross-sectional surveys, their additional value needs to be balanced against the fact that they have a very long payoff period in policy terms and are complex to analyze.

How can different surveys be more closely coordinated?

Existing instruments differ in many aspects, including the target populations, the breadth and depth of the measurement instruments, the analytic objectives, and the assessment methods. What steps could be undertaken to strengthen the coordination between different assessment and evaluation efforts? This question has several aspects:

How can different instruments be integrated conceptually? It will be important to ensure coherence in the assessment frameworks and assessment methods. While instruments such as TIMSS and PISA have a very different conceptual orientation – with TIMSS focusing on the common denominator of national curricula and PISA emphasizing a broader and cross-curricular approach to knowledge and skills – it is important to articulate the commonalities and differences between the two approaches so that given the costs, the benefits of participation become apparent to both the participants and users of these surveys. The conceptual coordination between PISA and TIMSS remains unsatisfactory. PISA and ALL have maintained some degree of conceptual consistency in the reading literacy domain by keeping a limited assessment pool in common. Nevertheless, much more progress is needed to fully capitalize on the synergies of the different assessment activities. In all these efforts, the framework established by DeSeCo can provide an important reference system for conceptually integrating existing and future assessments.

How can international and national assessments be more closely interrelated? It is of utmost importance to ensure that national and international assessments are closely integrated, both to ensure the best possible use of international results for national policy development and to minimize costs and response burdens on schools. Otherwise, there is the risk that both time and resource constraints will limit participation by countries and schools in these activities, to the detriment of this important work. While OECD countries have decided that PISA should not be driven by national curricula or their common denominator, for the interpretation of international benchmarks in the national context it is important for countries to understand where national curricula are situated within international assessments. In the longer term, explicit linkages and comparisons of international assessment results with national estimates could perhaps be sought through the inclusion of intact blocks of international assessment items in national assessments or vice versa.

How can the design and timing of international surveys be better coordinated? Insufficient coordination among different surveys has resulted in increased costs and duplication of operations in participating countries and placed a great burden on participating schools in terms of access to student response time and dealing with differences in assessment procedures. Further progress will depend not only on the international organizations, but also on OECD member countries, who ultimately decide on the priorities and timing of each of the surveys.

How can the operation and management of international surveys be more closely coordinated at both the national and international levels to maximize synergies and minimize the response burden and costs on countries? Issues of institutional structures and management also need to be addressed. PISA has set an example for international collaboration in the development and implementation of comparative assessments. Participating countries are shaping the program in various ways: As members of the Board of Participating Countries, they determine the policy objectives and broad design parameters for the assessment project and guide analysis and reporting; as participants in functional expert groups, they contribute to the development of the conceptual framework and the assessment instruments together with the contracted international consortium; and through National Project Managers, they implement the project at the national level subject to the agreed-upon administration procedures. Member countries also continue to engage in long-term development work and to ensure the coherence of the survey program over time. All countries contribute to the financing of international activities based on an agreed-upon formula. However, despite the obvious strengths and success of this management model, it will be important to consider for an overall coherent assessment program how this management model may be further developed and to review how country participation can be further strengthened.

Strengthening cooperation beyond OECD membership. While developed around OECD objectives and the needs of OECD countries, the OECD assessment strategy has, from the outset, been open to the participation of non-OECD countries, and an increasing number of non-OECD countries are taking advantage of this opportunity. Given the increasing number of applications from non-OECD countries and the need to deal with these appropriately in the analytic work and international publications, it would now be important to establish a more coherent strategic approach to maximize the benefit for the non-OECD countries and for the OECD assessment strategy as a whole.

To conclude, comparative assessments provide a useful tool to improve the knowledge base about the distribution of competencies among individuals, institutions, and countries. A key difficulty for those utilizing and interpreting results from assessments remains, however, that the decisions and assumptions that have been made in the design of the various assessments have often not been sufficiently transparent. Given the increasing normative impact that assessments are having, there is a risk that without recognition of their limitations, attention – and resources – in education systems will be diverted from outcomes that are important but that are not covered by the respective assessments.

DeSeCo's overarching frame of reference provides a way to situate assessments within a larger conceptual context and to recognize the limitations of current assessments. The three categories of key competencies guide the systematic extension of future assessment instruments toward capturing a wider range of competencies.

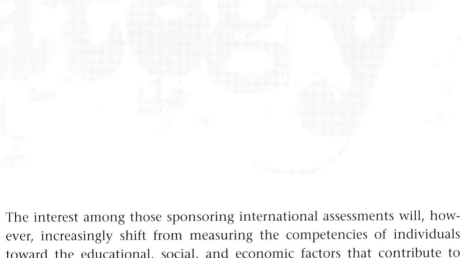

The interest among those sponsoring international assessments will, however, increasingly shift from measuring the competencies of individuals toward the educational, social, and economic factors that contribute to improved education and learning and to enhanced returns on investment in education in terms of personal, economic, and social well-being. The value of international assessments for policy development will thus increasingly depend on the analysis of the results and how effectively these analyses reach the relevant actors in various settings. Developing a framework to strengthen the analytic power of future assessments – as DeSeCo has strengthened the definition and conceptualization of competencies in relation to societal goals – now seems to be the next important task.

Concluding remarks

Heinz Gilomen

The ambitious journey we embarked on five years ago has come to an end. It has been – for the statistical agencies that took on this theory-oriented project – a rather unusual endeavor. Starting from the assumption that defining and selecting key competencies implies scientific discussion and analysis, practical considerations, and political processes and negotiations, we approached the topic of key competencies from multiple perspectives. Preparing to explore this uncharted territory, we assembled a heterogeneous group, including statisticians, economists, an anthropologist, sociologists, philosophers, psychologists, a historian, education researchers, policy-makers and policy analysts, unionists, and employers. Our task required considering the issues at stake from different viewpoints, understanding the different concerns brought to the table, keeping our minds open, and discovering new possibilities. We had to put aside many issues, and the various concerns and perspectives were simplified to some extent, but all the while a conscious effort was made to avoid falling into simplistic or reductionist analysis. Although the project originated in the context of assessment and indicator development and was carried out under the OECD INES Education Indicators Programme, the intent was that the project not be constrained by concerns of measurability and assessment of competencies. To be sure, such concerns are critical and regularly informed our efforts, yet they did not dictate the course or outcome of DeSeCo.

DeSeCo's work program was devised in response to an increased policy interest in education and learning outcomes and in recognition of the fact that high-quality information, data, and statistics are indispensable for social monitoring and effective policy-making. Within the framework of the modernization of educational systems – where objectives are gradually being redirected toward the results of teaching – as well as in the context of evaluating human capital, obtaining information about the competencies of students and adults has become a key issue in many policy sectors. One potential guiding framework for the development of indicators of competencies, in the sense of a limited number of extremely relevant statistics, is based on the concept of key competence. The fundamental hypothesis is that a small number of key competencies exist and play a particularly significant role in our ability to manage our lives. Thus, DeSeCo set out to explore this topic from a theory- and policy-oriented perspective and to provide answers to the following crucial questions:

- Is the basic hypothesis that a small number of key competencies exist correct?

- If so, what are these key competencies?

- To what extent do differences and convergences about the significance of key competencies exist in different political, economic, social, and cultural environments?

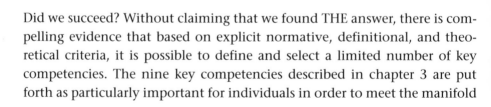

Did we succeed? Without claiming that we found THE answer, there is compelling evidence that based on explicit normative, definitional, and theoretical criteria, it is possible to define and select a limited number of key competencies. The nine key competencies described in chapter 3 are put forth as particularly important for individuals in order to meet the manifold global challenges facing them in a wide spectrum of contexts. For a project entitled *Definition and Selection of Competencies*, confirming the hypothesis outlined above might seem an adequate or satisfactory outcome.

Yet in light of the issues at stake, DeSeCo's mission was more extensive. Recognizing that a broad conceptual and theoretical foundation is essential for guiding the development of indicators of competencies and ensuring their sound interpretation, DeSeCo's efforts went beyond producing another list of key competencies and focused on identifying concepts and theoretical models that are meaningful to policy concerns and that can underpin the definition of competence and the construction of key competencies.

DeSeCo confirmed through the country contribution process (CCP) and commentaries from those in policy and practice that key competence is a concept with policy appeal in OECD countries. And we learned that in spite of the diversity of approaches, enough commonalities exist to enable the elaboration of a common frame of reference for key competencies. But we also observed that there was often little conceptual coherence to the discourse. DeSeCo succeeded in bringing some clarity to this conceptual confusion.

As illustrated in figure 1, DeSeCo's efforts resulted in an overarching frame of reference that can situate current and future key competencies in a larger conceptual context. It includes, as major elements, the concepts of competence and key competence based on various theoretical elements and models; a normative anchoring point; the specification of the nature of key competencies through the concept of reflectivity, grounded in an evolutionary developmental model and required by the complex mental demands of modern life; and the three-fold categorization for key competencies needed for a successful life and a well-functioning society. Key competencies are viewed as functioning not as independent entities, but as constellations of multiple interrelated key competencies that take on different forms depending on contextual or cultural factors.

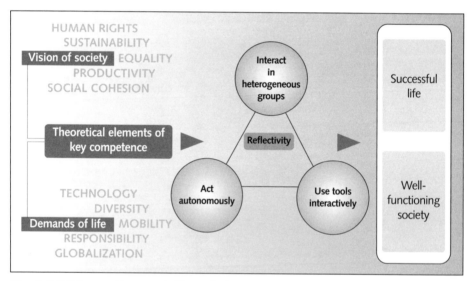

Figure 1: DeSeCo's overarching conceptual frame of reference
Source: DeSeCo

DeSeCo's work resulted in a panoply of implications for current and future theoretical and empirical work, and here I would like to highlight a few of them.

As discussed in this volume, challenges often associated with modern life such as dealing with diversity, taking responsibility, and navigating social space call for the development of a critical stance and a reflective approach to life. This reflectivity – a transversal feature of key competence – has important implications for both education and assessment. The underlying evolutionary model, in which mental development continues well into adulthood, provides a compelling rationale for lifelong learning and, furthermore, an important theoretical foundation for developing a coherent assessment strategy that spans youth and adults.

The nature of competence and key competence, as defined by DeSeCo, poses important challenges to assessments. For instance, the notion that key competencies function as constellations raises questions about current usage of assessments for benchmarking based on single measures. As assessments are developed in the future, it will be particularly important to recognize that key competencies do function together as constellations and to integrate and relate cognitive and noncognitive aspects of competence. Thus, to do justice to the complex nature of key competencies, to measure them validly and reliably, and to interpret the significance of the results with regard to multiple reference points, a variety of methods will need to be considered and explored. For example, profiles of competencies, instead of benchmarks, may have significant promise as an alternative strategy for interpreting results and for planning what to include in future studies. Also, relevant data may be derived from multiple sources, including, but not limited to, the collection of data through large-scale assessments.

As a last point, I would like to emphasize the importance of exploring conceptually and empirically the assumed linkages between key competencies and desired outcomes at both the micro and macro levels. If, as we have presumed, key competencies represent an educational response to today's global challenges and ongoing transformation processes and a strategic resource for sustainable socioeconomic development, understanding how they contribute to desired outcomes becomes a research topic of prime importance.

In this respect, much can be learned from the discipline of economics and human capital theory, where conceptual linkages between competencies and economic outcomes are well developed.

We recognize that DeSeCo's overarching frame of reference needs to be further refined through confrontation with empirical data and continued interdisciplinary research. Many of the findings delineated and elaborated in this volume – DeSeCo's final report – need to be and will be revisited, criticized, and refined by others as the process continues and the work moves "forward" and "outward" within and beyond the OECD. DeSeCo's approach of bringing together countries and experts from different disciplines, sectors, and organizations, and of organizing symposia as a means for debate, exploration, and reflection among a diverse audience is – I believe – an excellent model for maintaining a broad, interdisciplinary, and policy-relevant perspective on the topic.

The fulfillment of our hope and DeSeCo's potential requires the sustained commitment on the part of countries and international organizations to a collaborative research and development process as well as to the provision of adequate resources to assure that everyone acquires and maintains not only basic skills and learning foundations, but the key competencies that empower individuals to lead a successful life and to contribute to a well-functioning society. And in this sense, we echo Perrenoud's concern: "What is the point of defining [key] competencies unless it is to mobilize all the resources required to enable all citizens to acquire them, first and foremost those who are at present failing to acquire them?"

Afterword

Eugene H. Owen

DeSeCo goes to the heart of what it means to be a capable, responsible, and thoughtful human being in a society that strives for a viable and sustainable future for all. It is another, in a long series of leaps forward, of our attempts over the past 40 years to identify and measure what students and adults should know and be able to do.

The indicator context

The OECD Education Indicators Programme (INES) Project began in the late 1980s with the goal of establishing a system for the development and presentation of comparable indicators on education, focusing not only on characteristics of systems and schools but on learners' outcomes as well. By the 1990s, INES had advanced its focus from establishing networks and setting technical standards toward discussing the gaps in the data and, in the specific context of outcomes, determining what outcomes to measure and how to measure them.

OECD countries struggled to answer these questions, coming to the conclusion early on that across our countries, the goals of schooling are broader than academic development, and also that what we wanted to measure might encompass learning that potentially takes place outside of school. These conclusions influenced the data strategy that countries developed for collecting information on outcomes and the design of the Programme for International Student Assessment (PISA).

That cognitive domains such as reading, mathematics, and science were important outcomes on which to collect information in PISA was clear from the outset. However, it also soon became evident that PISA should have a component that focuses on measuring the less well defined outcomes, which include both cognitive and noncognitive aspects and which are not specific to any particular subject area. And although we had some basis of experience with a sampling of such cross-curricular competencies (e.g., civics, self-concept, problem-solving), the novelty of this area and the lack of an overarching conceptual frame of reference for thinking about it were apparent.

While indicator and assessment work continued, DeSeCo was launched to provide a solid theoretical base for the new competence domains by focusing on the broader notion of what competence and key competence mean in our societies and on what, from a theoretical, conceptual, and forward-looking perspective, we should be attempting to understand and measure.

Creating a vision for the future

Since the DeSeCo Project's inception, one of the main strengths of the project has been its extensive collaborative effort, which has sought input from a variety of academic, cultural, and practical perspectives. And in the end, the overarching conceptual framework that came out of the reflections, debates, and discussions among the participants resonated well with the project's stakeholders.

I'm particularly pleased that the three-fold categorization of key competencies – interacting in heterogeneous groups, acting autonomously, and using tools interactively – offers an organizing framework for domains such as reading, mathematics, and science. But it is critical to expand assessments into new, important domains. For this, the key competencies put forth in the three-fold categorization provide a valuable basis for discussion and consensus-building about which new competencies should and could be included in future international assessments.

DeSeCo has done an impressive job of mapping out, in a theoretically and conceptually sound way, the boundaries of these categories and of covering the range of activities we think of as important in today's world. Still, in order to ensure that what we measure internationally tomorrow is most relevant for our countries, we have several important steps ahead of us.

In one direction, we can tackle the specification of competencies within the DeSeCo framework, by fleshing out the contents of the categories and determining where in these categories, on these maps, we want to go and how we can get there. Developing the specific competencies within all three categories in ways that will be valid and meaningful across cultures – and contribute to informed decisions on issues related to human development policy – will be especially challenging.

In another direction, we can begin the task of identifying, as Heinz Gilomen has begun to reflect on in chapter 4, what the benefits of competencies are, both for individuals and for societies. Ultimately, this can affect our interpretation of the information gained from assessments and ensure that we understand the impact and importance of key competencies in leading our societies toward a more just and peaceful future.

Embarking on a bold adventure

When DeSeCo began in December 1997, it had both its supporters, who urged the need for solid conceptual foundations, and its skeptics, who wondered if it would ever be possible to identify competencies that have shared meaning and importance across the varied OECD contexts. There was a sense – among both the cautious and the optimistic – that we were beginning a bold adventure with an uncertain outcome.

While we hoped this adventure would yield a frame of reference from which indicator and assessment work could benefit, perhaps we did not realize at the time another potential benefit, the induction of a new and diverse group of contributors. When DeSeCo began, it was within the context of the INES Project and among a group of individuals who had long been working to develop internationally comparable indicators of outcomes. The impetus for the project came from the pioneers and sages of the OECD indicators work such as Norberto Bottani, Walo Hutmacher, and Uri Peter Trier. Over time, however, as the project was implemented, the group of "insiders" grew with the invitation of a host of new scholars from different spheres to participate and share in the work of the OECD and INES. As Scott Murray has noted in chapter 5, the establishment of this wide-ranging network of researchers, each of whom cares about the issue of competence from his or her own unique perspective, is a major accomplishment of the project and one of the keys to the extension and sustainability of its ideas in future endeavors.

Taking these next steps will be another bold adventure. Although the challenges ahead will be daunting, they are worth the effort because to do less would be to fall short of our vision of the important outcomes of teaching and learning.

References

Allardt, E. (1993). Having, loving, being: An alternative to the Swedish model of welfare research. In N. Nussbaum & A. Sen (Eds.), *The quality of life* (pp. 88–94). Oxford: Clarendon Press.

Baker, D.P., Horvath, L., Campion, M., Offermann, L., & Salas, E. (1999). *Teamwork: Status Memorandum* (Working draft). Retrieved May 27, 2003, from http://www.ets.org/all/

Binkley, M., Sternberg, R., Jones, S., & Nohara, D. (1999). An overarching framework for understanding and assessing life skills. In *Frameworks: Working drafts*. Briefing materials for Adult Literacy and Life Skills National Study Manager's Meeting. Luxembourg.

Bourdieu, P. (1979). *La distinction. La critique sociale du jugement*. Paris: Editions de Minuit.

Bourdieu, P. (1980). *Le sens pratique*. Paris: Editions de Minuit.

Bourdieu, P. (1982). *Ce que parler veut dire: L'économie des échanges linguistiques*. Paris: Fayard.

Bourdieu, P. (1983). Forms of capital. In J.G. Richardson (Ed.), *Handbook of theory and research for the sociology of education* (pp. 241–258). New York: Greenwood.

Brink, S. (2003). Policy research in support of the skills agenda of the government of Canada. In D.S. Rychen, L.H. Salganik, & M.E. McLaughlin (Eds.), *Selected contributions to the 2nd DeSeCo symposium*. Neuchâtel, Switzerland: Swiss Federal Statistical Office.

Callieri, C. (2001). The knowledge economy: A business perspective. In D.S. Rychen & L.H. Salganik (Eds.), *Defining and selecting key competencies* (pp. 228–231). Göttingen, Germany: Hogrefe & Huber.

Canto-Sperber, M., & Dupuy, J.P. (2001). Competencies for the good life and the good society. In D.S. Rychen & L.H. Salganik (Eds.), *Defining and selecting key competencies* (pp. 67–92). Göttingen, Germany: Hogrefe & Huber.

Carey, S. (Ed.). (1999). *The International Adult Literacy Survey in the European context.* London: United Kingdom National Office of Statistics.

Carson, J. (2001). Defining and selecting competencies: Historical reflections on the case of IQ. In D.S. Rychen & L.H. Salganik (Eds.), *Defining and selecting key competencies* (pp. 33–44). Göttingen, Germany: Hogrefe & Huber.

Coleman, J.S. (1988). Social capital in the creation of human capital. *American Journal of Sociology*, 94, 95–120.

Dahrendorf, R., Field, F., Hayman, C., & Hutcheson, I. (1995). *Report on wealth creation and social cohesion in a free society.* London: Commission on Wealth Creation and Social Cohesion.

Danish Federation of Trade Unions. (1999). *The national human capital account.* Copenhagen: Author.

Delors, J., & Draxler, A. (2001). From unity of purpose to diversity of expression and needs: A perspective from UNESCO. In D.S. Rychen & L.H. Salganik (Eds.), *Defining and selecting key competencies* (pp. 214–221). Göttingen, Germany: Hogrefe & Huber.

DeSeCo Project Web site. (2002). Retrieved May 27, 2003, from http://www.deseco.admin.ch

Dunon, R. (2001). *Definition and selection of key competencies in Belgium (Flanders).* Retrieved May 27, 2003, from http://www.statistik.admin.ch/stat_ch/ber15/deseco/sfso_deseco_ccp_belgium_19122001.pdf

Emin, J.-C. (2003). Proposal for a strategy to assess adults' competencies. In D.S. Rychen, L.H. Salganik, & M.E. McLaughlin (Eds.), *Selected contributions to the 2nd DeSeCo symposium.* Neuchâtel, Switzerland: Swiss Federal Statistical Office.

Erikson, R. (1993). Descriptions of inequality: The Swedish approach to welfare research. In N. Nussbaum & A. Sen (Eds.), *The quality of life* (pp. 67–83). Oxford: Clarendon Press.

Etelälahti, A., & Sahi, A. (2001). *Definition and selection of key competencies in Finland.* Retrieved May 27, 2003, from
http://www.statistik.admin.ch/stat_ch/ber15/deseco/sfso_deseco_ccp_finland_19122001.pdf

European Commission. (2001). *Communication from the Commission: Making a European area of lifelong learning a reality.* Brussels: Author. Retrieved May 27, 2003, from
http://europa.eu.int/comm/education/life

Farrugia, J.-P. (2001). Competence management as an investment: A business perspective. In D.S. Rychen & L.H. Salganik (Eds.), *Defining and selecting key competencies* (pp. 232–235). Göttingen, Germany: Hogrefe & Huber.

Featherman, D., & Carson, J. (1999). Commentary on *Concepts of competence*. In *Comments on the DeSeCo expert opinions* (pp. 89–90). Retrieved May 27, 2003, from
http://www.statistik.admin.ch/stat_ch/ber15/deseco/comments_deseco_expert_opinions.pdf

Fratczak-Rudnicka, B., & Torney-Purta, J. (2003). Competencies for civic and political life in a democracy. In D.S. Rychen, L.H. Salganik, & M.E. McLaughlin (Eds.), *Selected contributions to the 2nd DeSeCo symposium*. Neuchâtel, Switzerland: Swiss Federal Statistical Office.

Gal, I., Tout, D., van Groenestijn, M., Schmitt, M.J., & Manley, M. (1999). *Numeracy.* Princeton, NJ: Educational Testing Service. Retrieved May 27, 2003, from
http://www.ets.org/all/numeracy.pdf

Giddings, D., & Barr-Telford, L. (2000). *Skill development and public policy*. Paris: Organisation for Economic Co-operation and Development; Ottawa: Statistics Canada; and Washington, DC: National Center for Education Statistics.

Gilomen, H., Rychen, D.S., & Salganik, L.H. (2001). Concluding remarks. In D.S. Rychen & L.H. Salganik (Eds.), *Defining and selecting key competencies* (pp. 247–251). Göttingen, Germany: Hogrefe & Huber.

Goleman, D. (1996). *Emotional intelligence: Why it can matter more than IQ.* New York: Bantam.

Gonczi, A. (2003). Teaching and learning of the key competencies. In D.S. Rychen, L.H. Salganik, & M.E. McLaughlin (Eds.), *Selected contributions to the 2nd DeSeCo symposium.* Neuchâtel, Switzerland: Swiss Federal Statistical Office.

Goody, J. (2001). Competencies and education: Contextual diversity. In D.S. Rychen & L.H. Salganik (Eds.), *Defining and selecting key competencies* (pp. 175–189). Göttingen, Germany: Hogrefe & Huber.

Green, D.A., & Riddell, W.C. (2001). *Literacy, numeracy, and labour market outcomes in Canada.* Ottawa: Statistics Canada and Human Resources Development Canada.

Grob, U., & Maag Merki, K. (2001). *Überfachliche Kompetenzen. Theoretische Grundlegung und empirische Erprobung eines Indikatorensystems.* Berne, Switzerland: Peter Lang.

Habich, R., & Noll, H.-H. (1994). *Soziale Indikatoren und Sozialberichterstattung. Internationale Erfahrungen und gegenwärtiger Forschungsstand.* Paris: International Social Science Council.

Harris, B. (2001). Are all key competencies measurable? An education perspective. In D.S. Rychen & L.H. Salganik (Eds.), *Defining and selecting key competencies* (pp. 222–227). Göttingen, Germany: Hogrefe & Huber.

Haste, H. (2001). Ambiguity, autonomy, and agency: Psychological challenges to new competence. In D.S. Rychen & L.H. Salganik (Eds.), *Defining and selecting key competencies* (pp. 93–120). Göttingen, Germany: Hogrefe & Huber.

Heckman, J., & Vytlacil, E. (2000). *Identifying the role of cognitive ability in explaining the level of change in the return to schooling* (Working Paper 7820). Cambridge, MA: National Bureau of Economic Research.

Hutmacher, W., Cochrane, D., & Bottani, N. (2001). *In pursuit of equity in education: Using international indicators to compare equity policies.* Dordrecht, Netherlands: Kluwer Academic Publishers.

Inglehart, R. (1989). *Kultureller Umbruch. Wertewandel in der westlichen Welt.* Frankfurt am Main/New York: Campus.

Keating, D.P. (2003). Definition and selection of competencies from a human development perspective. In D.S. Rychen, L.H. Salganik, & M.E. McLaughlin (Eds.), *Selected contributions to the 2nd DeSeCo symposium*. Neuchâtel, Switzerland: Swiss Federal Statistical Office.

Kegan, R. (1994). *In over our heads: The mental demands of modern life*. Cambridge, MA: Harvard University Press.

Kegan, R. (2001). Competencies as working epistemologies: Ways we want adults to know. In D.S. Rychen & L.H. Salganik (Eds.), *Defining and selecting key competencies* (pp. 192–204). Göttingen, Germany: Hogrefe & Huber.

Kelly, F. (2001). *Definition and selection of key competencies in New Zealand*. Retrieved May 27, 2003, from
http://www.statistik.admin.ch/stat_ch/ber15/deseco/sfso_deseco_ccp_newzealand_19122001.pdf

Kerckhoff, A., Dietrich, E., & Brown, S. (2000). *Evaluating measures of educational attainment in comparative research* (Unpublished manuscript). Ottawa: Statistics Canada.

Kirsch, I.S. (2001). *The International Adult Literacy Survey (IALS): Understanding what was measured*. Princeton, NJ: Educational Testing Service. Retrieved May 27, 2003, from
http://www.ets.org/all/Prose_and_Doc_framework.pdf

Knain, E. (2001). *Definition and selection of key competencies in Norway*. Retrieved May 27, 2003, from
http://www.statistik.admin.ch/stat_ch/ber15/deseco/sfso_deseco_ccp_norway_19122001.pdf

Krahn, H., & Lowe, G.S. (1998). *Literacy utilization in Canadian workplaces*. Ottawa: Statistics Canada and Human Resources Development Canada.

L'Hardy, Ph., Guével, C., & Soleilhavoup, J. (Eds.). (1996). *La société française. Données sociales*. Paris: Institut National de la Statistique et des Etudes Economiques (INSEE).

Lassnigg, L. (1998). Description of the educational pathways in Austria. In *Pathways and participation in vocational and technical education and training* (pp. 81–116). Paris: OECD.

Lassnigg, L., Mayer, K., & Svecnik, E. (2001). *Definition and selection of key competencies in Austria.* Retrieved May 27, 2003, from http://www.statistik.admin.ch/stat_ch/ber15/deseco/sfso_deseco_ccp_austria_19122001.pdf

Lave, J., & Wenger, E. (1990). *Situated learning: Legitimate peripheral participation.* Cambridge: Cambridge University Press.

Le Boterf, G. (1994). *De la compétence: Essai sur un attracteur étrange.* Paris: Les Editions d'Organisation.

Le Boterf, G. (1997). *De la compétence à la navigation professionnelle.* Paris: Les Editions d'Organisation.

Levy F., & Murnane, R.J. (2001). Key competencies critical to economic success. In D.S. Rychen & L.H. Salganik (Eds.), *Defining and selecting key competencies* (pp. 151–173). Göttingen, Germany: Hogrefe & Huber.

Martin, J., & Pearson, M. (2001). *OECD social indicators: A broad approach towards social reporting.* Paris: OECD.

Maslow, A. (1954). *Motivation and personality.* New York: Harper.

Maslow, A. (1971). *The farther reaches of human nature.* New York: Viking Press.

Maslow, A., & Lowery, R. (Eds.). (1998). *Toward a psychology of being* (3rd ed.). New York: Wiley & Sons.

Merrifield, J. (2000). *Equipped for the future research report.* Washington, DC: National Institute for Literacy.

Ministère de l'Education Nationale, France. (2001). *Definition and selection of key competencies in France.* Retrieved May 27, 2003, from http://www.statistik.admin.ch/stat_ch/ber15/deseco/sfso_deseco_ccp_france_19122001.pdf

Murray, T.S. (1995). *Proxy measurement of adult basic skills: Lessons from Canada.* Philadelphia, PA: National Center on Adult Literacy, University of Pennsylvania.

Murray, T.S., Kirsch, I.S., & Jenkins, L. (Eds.). (1998). *Adult literacy in OECD countries: Technical report on the first International Adult Literacy Survey* (NCES 1998-053). U.S. Department of Education, National Center for Education Statistics. Washington, DC: U.S. Government Printing Office.

The National Commission on Civic Renewal. (1998). *A nation of spectators: How civic disengagement weakens America and what we can do about it.* Retrieved May 27, 2003, from
http://www.puaf.umd.edu/Affiliates/CivicRenewal/finalreport/table_of_contentsfinal_report.htm

National Commission on Excellence in Education. (1983). *A nation at risk: The imperative for educational reform.* Washington, DC: U.S. Government Printing Office.

National Education Goals Panel. (1999). *The national education goals report: Building a nation of learners.* Washington, DC: U.S. Government Printing Office.

Noll, H.-H. (1978). Soziale Indikatoren für Arbeitsmarkt und Beschäftigungsbedingungen. In W. Zapf (Ed.), *Lebensbedingungen in der Bundesrepublik. Sozialer Wandel und Wohlfahrtsentwicklung* (2nd ed., pp. 209–322). Frankfurt am Main: Campus.

Noll, H.-H. (2001). *Towards a European system of social reporting and welfare measurement.* The EuReporting Project. Final Report. Mannheim, Germany: The Centre for Survey Research and Methodology (ZUMA).

Oates, T. (1999). *Analysing and describing competence - critical perspectives.* Sudbury, England: Qualifications and Curriculum Authority.

Oates, T. (2003). Key skills/key competencies: Avoiding the pitfalls of current initiatives. In D.S. Rychen, L.H. Salganik, & M.E. McLaughlin (Eds.), *Selected contributions to the 2nd DeSeCo symposium.* Neuchâtel, Switzerland: Swiss Federal Statistical Office.

Oliva, A. (2003). Key competencies in and across social fields: The employers' perspective. In D.S. Rychen, L.H. Salganik, & M.E. McLaughlin (Eds.), *Selected contributions to the 2nd DeSeCo symposium.* Neuchâtel, Switzerland: Swiss Federal Statistical Office.

Organisation for Economic Co-operation and Development. (1976). *Mesure du bien-être social: Un rapport sur les progrès d'élaboration des indicateurs sociaux* (Working paper). Paris: Author.

Organisation for Economic Co-operation and Development. (1982). *The OECD list of social indicators.* Paris: Author.

Organisation for Economic Co-operation and Development. (1992). *Adult illiteracy and economic performance.* Paris: Author.

Organisation for Economic Co-operation and Development. (1999). *Measuring student knowledge and skills.* Paris: Author.

Organisation for Economic Co-operation and Development. (2000). *Measuring student knowledge and skills: The PISA 2000 assessment of reading, mathematical, and scientific literacy.* Paris: Author.

Organisation for Economic Co-operation and Development. (2001a). *Knowledge and skills for life: First results from PISA 2000.* Paris: Author.

Organisation for Economic Co-operation and Development. (2001b). *Meeting of the OECD Education Ministers, Paris, 3–4 April 2001: Investing in competencies for all (communiqué).* Retrieved May 27, 2003, from
http://www.oecd.org/pdf/M00008000/M00008906.pdf

Organisation for Economic Co-operation and Development. (2001c). *Society at a glance: OECD social indicators.* Paris: Author.

Organisation for Economic Co-operation and Development. (2001d). *The well-being of nations: The role of human and social capital.* Paris: Author.

Organisation for Economic Co-operation and Development. (2002). *Definition and Selection of Competencies (DeSeCo): Theoretical and Conceptual Foundations: Strategy paper.* Retrieved May 27, 2003, from
http://www.statistik.admin.ch/stat_ch/ber15/deseco/deseco_strategy_paper_final.pdf

Organisation for Economic Co-operation and Development & Human Resources Development Canada. (1995). *Literacy, economy and society.* Paris: OECD; and Ottawa: Human Resources Development Canada.

Organisation for Economic Co-operation and Development, Human Resources Development Canada, & Statistics Canada. (1997). *Literacy skills for the knowledge society: Further results of the International Adult Literacy Survey.* Paris: OECD; and Ottawa: Human Resources Development Canada and Statistics Canada.

Organisation for Economic Co-operation and Development & Statistics Canada. (1995). *Literacy, economy, and society: Results of the first International Adult Literacy Survey.* Paris: OECD; and Ottawa: Statistics Canada.

Organisation for Economic Co-operation and Development & Statistics Canada. (2000). *Literacy in the information age: Final report of the International Adult Literacy Survey.* Paris: OECD; and Ottawa: Statistics Canada.

Osberg, L. (2000). *Schooling, literacy, and individual earnings.* Ottawa: Statistics Canada and Human Resources Development Canada.

Otterstrom, A. (2001). *Definition and selection of key competencies in Denmark.* Retrieved May 27, 2003, from
http://www.statistik.admin.ch/stat_ch/ber15/deseco/sfso_deseco_ccp_denmark_19122001.pdf

Ouane, A. (2003). Defining and selecting key competencies in lifelong learning. In D.S. Rychen, L.H. Salganik, & M.E. McLaughlin (Eds.), *Selected contributions to the 2nd DeSeCo symposium.* Neuchâtel, Switzerland: Swiss Federal Statistical Office.

Perrenoud, P. (2001). The key to social fields: Competencies of an autonomous actor. In D.S. Rychen & L.H. Salganik (Eds.), *Defining and selecting key competencies* (pp. 121–149). Göttingen, Germany: Hogrefe & Huber.

Peschar, J.L. (2001). *Definition and selection of key competencies in the Netherlands.* Retrieved May 27, 2003, from
http://www.statistik.admin.ch/stat_ch/ber15/deseco/sfso_deseco_ccp_netherlands_19122001.pdf

Putnam, R.D. (Ed.). (2001). *Gesellschaft und Gemeinsinn: Sozialkapital im internationalen Vergleich.* Gütersloh, Germany: Bertelsmann-Stiftung.

Rawls, J. (1972). *A theory of justice.* New York: Oxford University Press.

Rekus, J., Hintz, D., & Ladenthin, V. (1998). *Die Hauptschule – Alltag, Reform, Geschichte, Theorie.* Weinheim/Munich, Germany: Juventa.

Ridgeway, C. (2001). Joining and functioning in groups, self-concept and emotion management. In D.S. Rychen & L.H. Salganik (Eds.), *Defining and selecting key competencies* (pp. 205–211). Göttingen, Germany: Hogrefe & Huber.

Riordan, T., & Rosas, G. (2003). Key Competencies: The ILO's perspective. In D.S. Rychen, L.H. Salganik, & M.E. McLaughlin (Eds.), *Selected contributions to the 2nd DeSeCo symposium.* Neuchâtel, Switzerland: Swiss Federal Statistical Office.

Ritchie, L. (2001). Key competencies for whom? A labor perspective. In D.S. Rychen & L.H. Salganik (Eds.), *Defining and selecting key competencies* (pp. 236–240). Göttingen, Germany: Hogrefe & Huber.

Rychen, D.S. (2001). Introduction. In D.S. Rychen & L.H. Salganik (Eds.), *Defining and selecting key competencies* (pp. 1–15). Göttingen, Germany: Hogrefe & Huber.

Rychen, D.S. (2003). A frame of reference for defining and selecting key competencies in an international context. In D.S. Rychen, L.H. Salganik, & M.E. McLaughlin (Eds.), *Selected contributions to the 2nd DeSeCo symposium*. Neuchâtel, Switzerland: Swiss Federal Statistical Office.

Rychen, D.S., & Salganik, L.H. (2000). Definition and selection of key competencies. In *The INES compendium: Contributions from the INES networks and working groups* (pp. 67–80). Paris: OECD.

Rychen, D.S., & Salganik, L.H. (Eds.). (2001). *Defining and selecting key competencies*. Göttingen, Germany: Hogrefe & Huber.

Rychen, D.S., & Salganik, L.H. (2002). *DeSeCo symposium: Discussion paper*. Retrieved May 27, 2003, from
http://www.statistik.admin.ch/stat_ch/ber15/deseco/deseco_discpaper_jan15.pdf

Salganik, L.H. (2001). Competencies for life: A conceptual and empirical challenge. In D.S. Rychen & L.H. Salganik (Eds.), *Defining and selecting key competencies* (pp. 17–32). Göttingen, Germany: Hogrefe & Huber.

Salganik, L.H. (2003). Highlights from current assessments. In D.S. Rychen, L.H. Salganik, & M.E. McLaughlin (Eds.), *Selected contributions to the 2nd DeSeCo symposium*. Neuchâtel, Switzerland: Swiss Federal Statistical Office.

Salganik, L.H, Rychen, D.S., Moser, U., & Konstant, J. (1999). *Projects on competencies in the OECD context: Analysis of theoretical and conceptual foundations*. Neuchâtel, Switzerland: Swiss Federal Statistical Office.

Schelsky, H. (1972). Die Bedeutung des Berufs in der modernen Gesellschaft. In T. Luckmann & W.M. Sprondel (Eds.), *Berufssoziologie* (pp. 25–35). Cologne, Germany: Kiepenheuer & Witsch.

Sen, A. (1987). *Commodities and capabilities*. New Delhi: Oxford University.

Sennett, R. (1998). *The corrosion of character: The transformation of work in modern capitalism*. New York: Norton.

Skolverket (National Agency for Education, Sweden). (2001). *Definition and selection of key competencies in Sweden*. Retrieved May 27, 2003, from http://www.statistik.admin.ch/stat_ch/ber15/deseco/sfso_deseco_ccp_sweden_19122001.pdf

Stein, S. (2000). *Equipped for the future content standards: What adults need to know and be able to do in the 21st century*. Washington, DC: National Institute for Literacy.

Stein, S. (2000). What family life demands: A purposeful view of competent performance. Washington, DC: National Institute for Literacy. In D.S. Rychen, L.H. Salganik, & M.E. McLaughlin (Eds.), *Selected contributions to the 2nd DeSeCo symposium*. Neuchâtel, Switzerland: Swiss Federal Statistical Office.

Street, B.V. (1999). The meanings of literacy. In D. Wagner, R. Venezky, & B.V. Street (Eds.), *Literacy: An international handbook*. Boulder, CO: Westview Press.

Stigler, J.W., Gonzales, P.A., Kawanka, T., Knoll, S., & Serrano, A. (1999). *The TIMSS Videotape Classroom Study: Methods and findings from an exploratory research project on eighth-grade mathematics instruction in Germany, Japan, and the United States* (NCES 1999–074). U.S. Department of Education, National Center for Education Statistics. Washington, DC: U.S. Government Printing Office.

Swartz, D. (1997). *Culture and power: The sociology of Pierre Bourdieu*. Chicago: University of Chicago Press.

Torney-Purta, J., Lehmann, R., Oswald, H., & Schulz, W. (2001). *Citizenship and education in twenty-eight countries: Civic knowledge and engagement at age fourteen*. Amsterdam: International Association for the Evaluation of Educational Achievement (Eburnon).

Trier, U.P. (2001a). Defining educational goals: A window to the future. In D.S. Rychen & L.H. Salganik (Eds.), *Defining and selecting key competencies* (pp. 241–246). Göttingen, Germany: Hogrefe & Huber.

Trier, U.P. (2001b). *Definition and selection of key competencies in Switzerland*. Retrieved May 27, 2003, from http://www.statistik.admin.ch/stat_ch/ber15/deseco/sfso_deseco_ccp_switzerland_19122001.pdf

Trier, U.P. (2001c). *Definition and selection of key competencies in the United States.* Retrieved May 27, 2003, from
http://www.statistik.admin.ch/stat_ch/ber15/deseco/sfso_deseco_ccp_us_19122001.pdf

Trier, U.P. (2003). Twelve countries contributing to DeSeCo: A summary report. In D.S. Rychen, L.H. Salganik, & M.E. McLaughlin (Eds.), *Selected contributions to the 2nd DeSeCo symposium.* Neuchâtel, Switzerland: Swiss Federal Statistical Office.

Tuijnman, A., & Bouchard, E. (2001). *Adult education participation in North America: International perspectives.* Ottawa: Statistics Canada and Human Resources Development Canada.

United Nations Conference on Environment and Development (UNCED). (1992). *Agenda 21, the Rio Declaration on Environment and Development.* New York: United Nations.

United Nations Division for Sustainable Development Web site. (2003). *Table 4: CSD [Commission on Sustainable Development] theme indicator framework.* Retrieved May 27, 2003, from
www.un.org/esa/sustdev/natlinfo/indicators/indisd/isdms2001/table_4.htm

United Nations Educational, Scientific and Cultural Organization (UNESCO). (1990). *World Declaration on Education for All: Meeting basic learning needs.* Retrieved May 27, 2003, from
http://www.unesco.org/education/efa/ed_for_all/background/jomtien_declaration.shtml

United Nations Educational, Scientific and Cultural Organization (UNESCO). (1996). *Learning: The treasure within.* Report to UNESCO of the International Commission on Education for the Twenty-First Century. Paris: Author.

United Nations Organization (UNO). (1948). *Universal Declaration of Human Rights.* General Assembly Resolution 217 A (III) of 10 December 1948. New York: Author.

U.S. Department of Labor. (1992). *Learning a living: A blueprint for high performance – A SCANS report for America 2000.* Washington, DC: The Secretary's Commission on Achieving Necessary Skills. Retrieved May 27, 2003, from
http://wdr.doleta.gov/SCANS/lal/LAL.htm

Verhasselt, E. (2002). *Literacy rules: Flanders and the Netherlands in the International Adult Literacy Survey.* Gent, Belgium: Academia Press.

Vogel, J., Andersson, G., Davidsson, U., & Häll, L. (1988). *Inequality in Sweden: Trends and current situation*. Stockholm: Statistics Sweden.

Weinert, F.E. (1999). *Concepts of competence*. Prepared for DeSeCo symposium 1999. Unpublished. Retrieved May 27, 2003, from
http://www.statistik.admin.ch/stat_ch/ber15/deseco/weinert_report.pdf

Weinert, F.E. (2001). Concept of competence: A conceptual clarification. In D.S. Rychen & L.H. Salganik (Eds.), *Defining and selecting key competencies* (pp. 45–65). Göttingen, Germany: Hogrefe & Huber.

Witt, R., & Lehmann, R. (2001). *Definition and selection of key competencies in Germany*. Retrieved May 27, 2003, from
http://www.statistik.admin.ch/stat_ch/ber15/deseco/sfso_deseco_ccp_germany_19122001.pdf

World Bank. (2002). *Lifelong learning in the global knowledge economy: Challenges for developing countries*. Retrieved May 27, 2003, from
http://www1.worldbank.org/education/pdf/Lifelong%20Learning_GKE.pdf

World Health Organization (WHO). (1946). Preamble to the constitution of the World Health Organization as adopted by the International Health Conference. In *Official records of the World Health Organization* (no. 2, p. 100). New York: Author.

Zapf, W. (1984). Individuelle Wohlfahrt: Lebensbedingungen und wahrgenommene Lebensqualität. In W. Glatzer & W. Zapf (Eds.), *Lebensqualität in der Bundesrepublik. Objektive Lebensbedingungen und subjektives Wohlbefinden*. Frankfurt am Main/New York: Campus.

Zapf, W. (1993). Wohlfahrtsentwicklung und Modernisierung. In W. Glatzer (Ed.), *Einstellungen und Lebensbedingungen in Europa* (pp. 163–176). Frankfurt am Main/NewYork: Campus.

Biographical notes

Heinz Gilomen is the Director of Social and Education Statistics at the Swiss Federal Statistical Office and a member of its board of directors. He is responsible for statistics relating to education and science as well as for social reporting and social indicators. He is the National Coordinator for the OECD Education Indicators Programme (INES) in Switzerland and the chair of the DeSeCo Steering Group.

Barry McGaw is the Director of the Directorate for Education in the OECD. His research interests have been in educational measurement and learning, with an emphasis on curriculum and assessment in the upper secondary years. His current work with the OECD includes an investigation of the role of national qualifications frameworks in recognizing and rewarding learning and a study of ways to increase incentives for individuals and enterprises to invest in continuing education and training.

T. Scott Murray is the Director of Social and Institutional Statistics, at Statistics Canada. Prior to his appointment to this position in 1999, he spent more than 20 years in the Special Surveys Division, including 5 years as Director. He has specialized in the design and conduct of large-scale ad hoc surveys to meet emerging public policy issues. His work has included studies of child care usage, longitudinal labor market activity, and international comparative work in the area of the assessment of adult skill.

Eugene H. Owen is the Director of the International Activities Program of the National Center for Education Statistics, U.S. Department of Education. He oversees planning and implementation of international assessments and studies in the United States, and is responsible for collecting and reporting statistical and qualitative information on education systems at the international level. He is the Chair of the INES Project's Network A, which focuses on learner outcomes, and of the PISA Board of Participating Countries.

Dominique Simone Rychen is a Senior Program Officer at the Swiss Federal Statistical Office and the Program Manager of the DeSeCo Project. She has been responsible for coordinating the various research activities within DeSeCo and reporting the findings to the OECD. She is co-editor, with Laura Hersh Salganik, of *Defining and Selecting Key Competencies* (Hogrefe & Huber, 2001). Previously, she worked on indicator development related to continuing education, labor market, workplace, and informal learning.

Laura Hersh Salganik is the Director of the Education Statistics Services Institute of the American Institutes for Research. Her areas of specialty include education indicators and international comparisons of education systems, and she has participated in numerous activities in the INES Project during the past 10 years. She is co-editor, with Dominique Simone Rychen, of *Defining and Selecting Key Competencies* (Hogrefe & Huber, 2001).

Andreas Schleicher is the Head of the Indicators and Analysis Division of the OECD's Directorate for Education. His responsibilities include managing PISA, the INES Project, and the OECD/UNESCO World Education Indicators Programme, and coordinating the development and implementation of education indicators and analyses with other international organizations. He was recently awarded the Theodor Heuss Award in Germany.

Maria Stephens is a Research Analyst at the American Institutes for Research. She has been involved in the INES Project and PISA since 1997, through her role managing the technical support provided to INES Network A and to the Chair of the PISA Board of Participating Countries. In this capacity, she has coordinated various Network A activities, worked on indicator development related to learner outcomes, and participated in strategic planning activities for PISA.